The *New* GAME *of* LIFE

AND HOW TO PLAY IT

OTHER TITLES IN THE

LIBRARY OF
HIDDEN KNOWLEDGE

The New Master Key System

The New Science of Getting Rich

Natural Abundance

Coming in 2012

As We Think, So We Are

LIBRARY OF
HIDDEN KNOWLEDGE

The *New* GAME of LIFE

AND HOW TO PLAY IT

the original text by

FLORENCE SCOVEL SHINN

edited by RUTH L. MILLER

ATRIA BOOKS
New York London Toronto Sydney New Delhi

BEYOND WORDS
Hillsboro, Oregon

ATRIA BOOKS
A Division of Simon & Schuster, Inc.
1230 Avenue of the Americas
New York, NY 10020

BEYOND WORDS
20827 N.W. Cornell Road, Suite 500
Hillsboro, Oregon 97124-9808
503-531-8700 / 503-531-8773 fax
www.beyondword.com

Managing editor: Lindsay S. Brown
Editor: Gretchen Stelter
Copyeditor: Meadowlark Publishing Services
Proofreaders: Susan Lynch, Jennifer Weaver-Neist
Design: Devon Smith
Composition: William H. Brunson Typography Services

First Atria Books/Beyond Words hardcover edition September 2012

For more information about special discounts for bulk purchases, please contact Simon & Schuster Special Sales at 1-866-506-1949 or business@simonandschuster.com.

The Simon & Schuster Speakers Bureau can bring authors to your live event. For more information or to book an event, contact the Simon & Schuster Speakers Bureau at 1-866-248-3049 or visit our website at www.simonspeakers.com.

Manufactured in the United States of America

10 9 8 7 6 5 4 3 2

Library of Congress Cataloging-in-Publication Data

Shinn, Florence Scovel, d. 1940.
    The new game of life and how to play it / Florence Scovel Shinn ; edited by
Ruth L. Miller.
        p.   cm.
Includes bibliographical.
    1. Shinn, Florence Scovel, d. 1940. Game of life and how to play it.
2. Success—Psychological aspects.   3. New Thought.   4. Spirituality.   5. Conduct of
life.   I. Miller, Ruth L., 1948–   II. Shinn, Florence Scovel, d. 1940. Game of life and
how to play it.   III. Title.
BF637.S8S5173   2012
158.1—dc23

                                                                                2012012559

ISBN 978-1-58270-374-9
ISBN 978-1-4516-7284-8 (ebook)

The corporate mission of Beyond Words Publishing, Inc.: *Inspire to Integrity*

Contents

A Note from the Editor   vii

Introduction   ix

INTERPRETATIONS
Modernized for the Twenty-First-Century Reader

1   The Game   3

2   The Principle of Prosperity   17

3   The Power of Words   29

4   The Principle of Nonresistance   41

5   Karma and the Principle of Forgiveness   53

6   Casting the Burden   67

7   The Principle of Love   83

8   Intuition as Guidance   95

9   Our Perfect Self-Expression—The Divine Design   109

10   Wealth and Well-Being   123

Some Effective Affirmations   137

A Summary of the Principles   141

Science Relating to *The Game of Life*   143

Notes   153

ORIGINAL TEXT
As Published in 1925

1 The Game   161

2 The Law of Prosperity   169

3 The Power of the Word   175

4 The Law of Nonresistance   181

5 The Law of Karma and the Law of Forgiveness   189

6 Casting the Burden (Impressing the Subconscious)   197

7 Love   205

8 Intuition or Guidance   213

9 Perfect Self-Expression or the Divine Design   221

10 Denials and Affirmations   229

Denials and Affirmations   237

A Note from the Editor

Florence Scovel Shinn wrote in a comfortable, colloquial style. She drew heavily on examples that matched the experience of the readers of her time but that don't always make sense to the twenty-first-century reader. In creating this updated version, I've used quotations from a variety of spiritual traditions as well as some modern terms and concepts (for example, nuclear power) that didn't exist in her day but make her points relevant to our current experience. The Unity tradition in which she worked says that all spiritual traditions contain the whole *perennial philosophy* but that each one offers its own perspective and teaching: they're unique paths leading to the same central core. While her audience wasn't aware of much beyond the Judeo-Christian perspective, we are, and I've honored that fact here by bringing in teachings from other traditions. Similarly, while she described situations using electricity and telephones back in 1925, later inventions are my additions.

This intermixing of modern ideas with her older text may be a little confusing for some readers because much of what she says is expressed in the first person, as "I was seeking an opportunity . . ." My advice is to envision that she's sitting here with you today, in the twenty-first century, because what Florence Scovel Shinn had to say is timeless; it's as useful now as it was almost a hundred years ago when she was writing it.

You may find it easiest to read the whole first section, the updated version, first. You may wish to do some of the exercises at the end of each chapter to get a feel for what she's teaching and then read her original text, which is the second section of the book. You can also go back and forth between her language and examples in the original text and the updated version, to make comparisons or choose which version of a particular point resonates best with you.

At the end of the first section you'll find a list of the statements, which she called affirmations, that she used to help her students and clients change their habits of thought. These have been pulled from the text to make them easy to access as you move through your own Game of Life. There's also a list, with definitions, of the Spiritual Principles she refers to in the text and relied on for transforming different situations. Most of these principles are explained in the text as well. Finally, before you get to her original text, you'll find a brief overview of experimental research done over the past fifty years supporting the principles and methods she put forth in this book.

You are about to embark on a remarkable journey of discovery. There are tools offered here that, if applied as directed, can completely transform your life. May you be empowered and enthused along the way!

Ruth L. Miller

INTRODUCTION

What Is the Game of Life?

There's a new kind of understanding emerging about how the world works, an understanding that's based on ancient ideas. The evidence no longer justifies the popular belief that we live in a dog-eat-dog world, one of continuous struggle for survival—in fact, cooperation and symbiosis appear to be the norm in the natural world, rather than competition and mutual destruction.

At the same time, more and more people are becoming aware of the power that our own mental model of the world has in shaping our lives and influencing the world around us. Through the popular writings of such famous doctors and therapists as Deepak Chopra and Wayne Dyer, and the powerful teachings of films like *Pay It Forward* and *The Secret*, many people are beginning to realize that what we think about profoundly influences what we experience.

This is not a new idea. In fact, it's been present in the many sacred texts of the world for thousands of years. The American philosopher Ralph Waldo Emerson brought this way of thinking into the industrialized world in the mid-1800s, and many schools of thought have since grown from his work.

The original author of this book, Florence Scovel Shinn, was profoundly influenced by Emerson's ideas. Applying them in her own life, she got powerful results and wanted to help others use them. In order to do so, she decided to help people shift from the "battle" model of life to a healthier, less destructive model and came up with the idea of a game as the easiest, most effective way to understand and apply the methods she was recommending.

As she conceived it, the Game of Life is a series of actions you can take to move from a life of lack and dis-ease to one of wealth and well-being, which she called Completion. Completion of the Game comes when we've achieved well-being in the four main areas of life—Health, Wealth, Love, and Perfect Self-Expression—through the mastery of Spiritual Principles.

In modern times, with so many of us playing video games, the idea of life as a great game is even more appropriate. This game is one in which, at each level, we follow clues and develop skills and understandings that allow us to move on to the next level. No matter where we start, we can find a principle or idea that will help us overcome the obstacles at that level, practice it in a variety of situations, and achieve a new level of accomplishment. Then we find new clues, new principles, and new ways of applying them that help us move to an even greater level of fulfillment. The difference between Shinn's Game of Life and the average video game, however, is that it gets simpler as we move from level to level, rather than more difficult. Now isn't that refreshing?

What Is New Thought?

Shinn studied with Emma Curtis Hopkins, "the teacher of teachers" in a peculiarly American spiritual movement called New

Thought,[1] during the 1910s and early '20s. Hopkins had a school in Chicago during the 1880s and '90s where she taught thousands of people her unique integration of Emerson's ideas with ancient mystical and spiritual traditions, along with the mental healing methods developed in the mid-1800s by Phineas Parkhurst Quimby of Maine. During the last few years of her life, Hopkins lived each winter in New York, and Shinn met her there.

Hopkins taught that when we look closely at the various spiritual traditions of the world, we realize that they all offer paths to a mental and physical state of peace and well-being. From the guidelines in the most ancient text, the Hindu Vedas, to the teachings of the most modern, the Qur'an, we've been offered ways of thinking and acting that will lift us out of the cultural programming of the subconscious mind and into the freedom of the superconscious mind, allowing us to live in harmony with our true nature.

The differences between these various teachings are primarily in the specific methods used. These differences are a result of the times and places in which the guidelines were offered—the culture of the teacher and the audience. The path of yoga, for instance, was introduced in a time and place where a few people could separate themselves from the day-to-day activities of life and still meet their needs. Though often misunderstood in the Western world, the path of jihad was introduced at a time when people had to strive mightily to avoid being swept up by the many conflicting ideas being promoted around them. Both of these paths have helped millions of people let go of thoughts and feelings that no longer serve them and shift their attention to the ever-present good that surrounds and sustains all of us.

Today, in a time where most people's needs are met, not in small communities or directly through their own work but through managing their finances, and when there's a constant stream of information available from television, magazines, newspapers, and the internet, these older methods don't always apply. To experience the good—the wealth, well-being, and peace— that is already ours, we must find a new set of methods for our time and place. This means we must build on the profound understandings of previous teachings and take them to the next level. We must bring the deep insight and knowing that are found at the heart of the world's spiritual traditions into a new language and form.

The key lies within. To overcome the patterns of today's world we must first transform our fundamental feelings and thoughts. And thought is often words—words spoken silently, internally, and spoken out loud, to ourselves or in the presence of others. This, then, must be the focus of our spiritual lives: to manage our thoughts and words in order to experience the truth of our being. We replace old, no longer useful thoughts with a new one—hence the name of the movement: New Thought.

The New Thought movement began in the late 1800s when Hopkins's students, Charles and Myrtle Fillmore, formed the Unity School and the Society of Silent Help. These grew into the Unity Association, with hundreds of centers and churches. Other Hopkins students formed what is now the International Divine Science Federation along with several dozen Homes and Sanctuaries of Truth. Emma's last student was Ernest Holmes, who founded the Institute of Religious Science in Los Angeles, now known as International Centers for Spiritual Living. Together with a few independents (such as Michael Beckwith's Agape Center in the Los Angeles area), these now number more than two thousand churches and centers around the world and continue to offer books, magazines, classes, online materials, and prayer support for anyone who calls, emails, or writes.

Who Was Florence Scovel Shinn?

Not a lot is known about this remarkable woman, but what we do know gives us glimpses of someone who was at the leading edge of her society, exploring new things and trying new ways of being at a time when the world was going through unimaginable changes.

Florence Scovel was born September 24, 1871, in Camden, New Jersey, to a family with a history going back to the Biddles, who arrived on the *Mayflower* more than two hundred fifty years before. During her childhood, the country was still reeling from the effects of the Civil War and her family was restoring its financial security. Though they were not wealthy, they provided her with a comfortable life and a fine education, and she grew up to be a strong, beautiful woman with flowing dark hair and lovely eyes.

In her late teens she attended the Pennsylvania Academy of the Fine Arts, where she excelled in drawing and illustration. It was there that she met the man who would become her husband, the artist Everett Shinn. Born in 1876, Everett was several years younger, but they had much in common, including a desire to make it big in the exciting city that would soon become known as the Big Apple.

After they married in 1898, they moved into an apartment on Waverly Place, near Washington Square and Greenwich Village in New York City. Almost immediately Everett launched a theater in the building next door and wrote three plays. No one was surprised when he cast his lovely wife in leading roles. He later became a member of the Ashcan School, also known as "the Eight," a group of revolutionary artists in the Greenwich Village area who were pushing the edges of what was considered acceptable as art.

For most of her life, Florence worked as an illustrator, so when she and Everett divorced in 1912, the forty-one-year-old relied on her artwork as her only means of support. Illustration didn't pay a lot, but she had long been part of a circle of artists and playwrights who were used to getting by on little and sharing much. Many of them also regularly visited and studied with the amazing healer and teacher named Emma Curtis Hopkins.

As often happens when people go through major life changes, Florence began to search for a deeper explanation of life. She found many answers, as well as powerful methods, in Hopkins's lessons. She soon found a place that offered similar teachings on a continuing basis: the New York Unity Society. There she met Dr. Emilie Cady, another student of Hopkins, whose book *Lessons in Truth* was already a foundation text for the Unity Institute. Shinn thus became part of a different kind of community: a group of people who had proved to themselves that their feelings and thoughts shaped their experience and that the spoken word is the means by which people receive the good, and not so good, things in life.

In time, Florence became a Unity teacher and offered classes and treatments for a fee. Her treatments helped people heal their bodies, their finances, and their relationships. They were based on the New Thought practice of *entering the silence*, a form of meditation in which we feel connected with the omnipotent source of all being, and from that space *speak the word*: express clearly the highest good about a situation so that both the speaker and the listener can experience it. The resulting manifestations of this highest good are often called *demonstrations*. Income from this work nicely supplemented her illustration contracts and so Florence was able to support herself for several decades.

After a number of years of increasing success as a healer and what we would today call a life coach, Florence's students persuaded her to write a book to more widely share her approach to the tools and techniques she'd learned. A new phase in her life began in 1925 when she arranged to have her manuscript typeset and printed, self-publishing the book that became her classic: *The Game of Life and How to Play It.*

The book was perfectly timed; 1925 was a year of major transition for the emerging New Thought movement and there was a need for what she had to offer. Her teacher, Emma Hopkins, was no longer writing or lecturing and passed on in April of that year; and Ernest Holmes published his classic *The Science of Mind* in June of the same year. In many ways, Shinn's *Game* and Holmes's *Science* were perfect complements to each other, his providing a comprehensive philosophy and hers providing simple, down-to-earth examples. Both were self-published and promoted in the many New Thought magazines and newsletters produced at the time. And both touched hearts and minds across the country with their clear expressions of truths that could transform lives.

Over the next several years, Shinn produced two other books, *Your Word Is Your Wand* and *The Secret Door to Success*, but focusing as they did on the need for mental discipline, neither caught the public's imagination as her *Game of Life* did—and still does today. The book has never been out of print since the first edition.

We know little more about Shinn's personal life. If she had children, she never discussed it in print. It's unlikely that she remarried, but we don't even know that for sure. We do know, however, that Florence passed on from what she would call the physical plane on October 17, 1940, just as New York was beginning to feel the effects of World War II. She had seen the invention of the bicycle, the motorcar, electricity, radio, the telephone, the airplane, and so much more. When she was a child, there were few paved streets and buildings were rarely more than four stories tall; by the time she passed on, New York City and its vicinity had become a vast network of streets and avenues weaving around the first skyscrapers and crawling with cars, trucks, and motorcycles. She had been part of the avant-garde culture of New York through World War I, Prohibition, and the Depression, and had personally helped many men and women find their way and work out their livelihoods through those difficult times.

The Essential Teaching

Florence Shinn was a powerful healer and teacher, and her work offers ideas and processes that we can use today. She drew heavily on both the Judeo-Christian biblical tradition and the traditions of the ancient mystery schools, using some concepts that may be unfamiliar to the modern reader. One of these is the term *square of life*, which she also refers to as *four-square* or *four-sided square*, and which has been used since ancient times to suggest completion, wholeness, and perfection—a four-sided pyramid (tetrahedron) being the ultimate example of completed growth.[2] Another is the previously mentioned *speaking the word*, which is pulled from a New Testament story in which a Roman centurion approaches Jesus the Nazarene and says, "Speak thou the word and my servant is healed." The expected result of speaking the word is a *demonstration*, which is the experience in material form of the idea spoken.

Her teachings were based on a very clear idea: all the good that is to be made manifest in our lives is already an accomplished fact in the universal Divine Mind and is experienced through our recognition and our spoken word. This is the fundamental idea of all New Thought teachings, and all the methods that Shinn and other teachers and practitioners offer are to help us recognize the truth that already exists so it may become our experience.

Shinn's work helped shape the language that is common across the various organizations that make up the New Thought movement and formed some of the basis for the best-selling book and film *The Secret*. Her work is also fundamental to the twelve-step program Adult Children of Alcoholics (ACOA). Through her books and the transformations that those she worked with experienced, she left a legacy that changes lives even today. Her methods continue to help people improve their lives, as many people who are part of the New Thought movement or have been through programs for ACOA are gratefully aware . . . and as we trust you'll experience in the following pages.

INTERPRETATIONS

*Modernized for the
Twenty-First-Century Reader*

1

THE GAME

Most people consider life a battle. It's not a battle, though; it's a game. And like most games, it can't be played successfully without understanding the rules.

For most of the games we learn to play, the rules outline specific actions we can or cannot execute to complete the game's process. They're taught in schools, written up in "cheat sheets," or learned from other players. For this game, however, the rules aren't so obvious. For the Game of Life, they're actually hidden carefully—in the one place, so the legend goes, that humanity would never look for it.[1] And as happens with any good video game, we're expected to discover them as we go along. We try things, and when we pay attention, we discover the pattern.

There actually is a secret cheat sheet, though. In this game, the rules are called Spiritual Principles, and the guide to them can be found in the sacred scriptures of the world, including the Hindu Vedic texts (especially the Bhagavad Gita), the Chinese Tao Te Ching, the Muslim Qur'an, the Jewish Torah, and the Christian New Testament.

In the Hindu scriptures—our most ancient written sacred texts—the Game of Life is taught as overcoming the law of Karma: whoever gives out hate will receive hate, whoever gives love will receive love, whoever criticizes will receive criticism, whoever lies will be lied to, and whoever cheats will be cheated.

As the New Testament describes, Jesus taught that the Game of Life was a great, ongoing process of giving and receiving, telling us that whatever we sow, we shall reap. This means that whatever anyone sends out into the universe, as word or deed, will return. Whatever we give out with intense emotion, we receive multiplied. When we *speak the word*—that is, say with feeling what we truly believe—we shall experience it.

The Muslim tradition encourages reliance on the divine for guidance through the Game; the opening to the Qur'an says, "Show us the straight way, the way of those on whom You [Allah] have bestowed Your Grace, those whose portion is not wrath, and who do not go astray."[2]

And in the Taoist tradition, the ancient master Lao Tse tells us in the Tao Te Ching that the Way—which is what *Tao* means—is beyond names but has clear principles. He asks us, "Can you love people and run things, and do so by not doing?"[3] The more we do, he says throughout the text, the more consequences we have to deal with.

Imagination: A Key Factor

Whatever spiritual tradition we follow, as we play the Game of Life and learn how all this works, we discover that imagination, our ability to make up and see images in our minds, plays a leading part in how the Game unfolds for us. Our imagination is forever shaping the pictures we see inside, and sooner or later we meet our own creations in our outer world.

I know of a man who feared a certain disease. It was a very rare disease and difficult to get, but he pictured it continually and read about it until it manifested in his body. He died the victim of his own distorted imagination.

We begin to find that whatever we imagine almost always becomes our circumstance.

So to play the Game of Life successfully, we need to learn how to train the imagination. People who train the mind to see only good bring all the good they can imagine into their lives—health, wealth, love, friends, Perfect Self-Expression—and their highest ideals come into form, compared to people who see unpleasant things.

A woman I know often pretended as a child that she was a widow. For years, she dressed up in black clothes and wore a long black veil, and people thought she was clever and amusing. She grew up and married someone she was deeply in love with. Sadly, he died not long after they were married, and she wore black with a sweeping veil for many years.

The inner picture of herself from childhood worked itself out in her life, regardless of the havoc and pain it created.

Understanding the Mind

To train the imagination successfully, it helps to understand the workings of our mind. Hindus call the Path of Knowledge *raja yoga*, which means the Kingly Path; to them, the mind is the king of our psychophysical structure. It's also why the Greeks said, "Know thyself" and posted it over the doorway of the temple at Delphi, where people went to receive guidance, and it's why the

Zen masters teach that we can "be the master of mind rather than be mastered by mind."

Carl Jung took this instruction seriously and studied the mind intensively for decades. He finally decided that there are three departments of the mind: the subconscious, the conscious, and the superconscious.

The subconscious is simply power without its own direction. Like computers and cell phones, it does what it's directed to do. It has no reasoning ability; it can't figure out if a symbol or word doesn't really mean what it says, nor does it logically filter through complex circumstances. Whatever anyone says powerfully, feels deeply, or imagines clearly is impressed upon the subconscious mind like a computer program, and like a computer, the subconscious carries out that program in precise detail. Sigmund Freud called this part of our mind the *id*, from the Latin for *it*. Most spiritual traditions call it our animal nature. Medical intuitive Caroline Myss and microbiologist Candace Pert both say that our body is our subconscious mind.

The conscious mind is sometimes called the mortal or carnal mind, or our Adam nature. Freud called it *ego*, from the Latin for *I*, and in his book *The Sacred Self* Wayne Dyer calls it our small self.[4] It's our normal, waking mind, and it sees life through the filters of our senses, language, and training. This aspect of our mind perceives only evidence for what it was trained to believe—which for most of us today includes death, disaster, sickness, poverty, and limitation of every kind—and it programs the subconscious to act accordingly.

The superconscious mind is often called the Higher Self, the Soul, or the Spirit within. It's the realm of perfect ideas. Freud called it the superego and Dyer calls it the Sacred Self. Some say it's the God Mind, Christ Mind, or Buddha Nature within each person. In the Hindu tradition, it's the *Atman*; Wiccans say it's the

Goddess. It's the light-filled core of our being, our essential nature, never separated from and always fully supplied by the ground of being, the Creator-Source of All. It's generally referred to as the Self, the capital S distinguishing it from the normal waking self or ego.

These three aspects of mind are always working together. One of the objects of the Game of Life is to reprogram the subconscious so that its operating system, the software that coordinates how our individual programs are acted out, is based on eternal and effective Spiritual Principles rather than the limiting beliefs we've adopted and built up in our conscious mind over the course of our lives.

Destiny and the Superconscious

Medieval Sufi mystic poet Jalal al-Din Rumi said, "Everyone has been made for some particular work, and the desire for that work has been put in every heart."[5] Several hundred years before that, the Apostle Paul told his assistant Timothy, "There is a place that you are to fill and no one else can fill, something you are to do, which no one else can do."[6] Krishna, as the embodiment of the Divine, said something very similar to Prince Arjuna in the Bhagavad Gita (the title means "Song of God," and it's often simply called "the Gita"), telling him that since he was a prince among warriors, "There is no better engagement for you than fighting on religious principles; and so there is no need for hesitation ... when you act in such knowledge you can free yourself from the bondage of works."[7]

The superconscious mind holds this ideal, this "perfect pattern." It's the Divine Design that Plato wrote about in *Timaeus*, his explanation of how the world works. All sacred traditions tell us there is a Divine Design for each of us, a particular form of

Perfect Self-Expression that no one else can do or have. It usually flashes across the conscious mind as an unattainable ideal, too good to be true. In reality it is our true destiny—our destination—flashed to us from the Infinite Intelligence, which is within the core of our very Self, in the form of our superconscious mind.

Many people, however, are unaware of their true destinies. Instead, they strive for things and situations that don't really belong to them, too often seeking what would only bring them failure and dissatisfaction if attained. All the spiritual traditions warn us against this trap, but still some people insist.

A woman came to me and asked me to speak the word that she would marry a certain someone with whom she was very much in love. (Let's call him A. B.) I replied that this would be a violation of Spiritual Principle, but that I would speak the word for the right man, the man who belonged to her by divine right. I added, "If A. B. is the right man, you can't lose him, and if he isn't, you will receive the equivalent." She saw A. B. frequently but no headway was made in their friendship.

One evening she called and said, "Do you know, for the last week, A. B. hasn't seemed so wonderful to me."

I replied, "Maybe he isn't the divine selection; someone else may be the right one."

Soon after that, she met someone who fell in love with her at once and who said she was his ideal. In fact, he said all the things that she had always wished A. B. would say to her. She told me, "It was quite uncanny." She soon returned his love and lost all interest in A. B.

This example shows the Principle of Substitution. She gave up her insistence that a specific person would fulfill her dreams and allowed a right idea to be substituted for a wrong one, so her

desire was fulfilled with no loss or sacrifice experienced by anyone involved. Had she insisted on her first choice, much distress
may have followed, as we shall see in a later example. The essence
of the principle is to substitute qualities for specific objects or
people in the desired experience.

The Principle of Substitution has long been spoken of in
sacred literature. In the Hebrew Bible, Solomon asked his God
for wisdom and was granted all riches and victory as well. In the
New Testament, Jesus said, "Seek first the Kingdom of God and
His righteousness and all these things shall be added unto you."
He went on to say that the Kingdom was within us. In the Gita,
Krishna, embodying the divine soul or Atman, said, "If a man
will ... meditate on me with an undistracted mind, devoting
every moment to me, I shall supply all his needs and protect his
possessions from loss."[8]

The Kingdom that Jesus speaks of and the Hindu Atman
refers to is the superconscious, the realm of right ideas and Plato's
Divine Design. When we focus on experiencing that more fully,
all the rest of life's gifts manifest effortlessly and joyfully.

We Need to Ask

There's always plenty of everything we need on our pathway, but
it can only be brought into our experience through our clear
intention, our understanding faith, and our spoken word. In the
Hebrew Bible, the prophet Isaiah heard the Voice of God saying,
"Concerning the works of my hands, command ye me."[9] Jesus
told us clearly that we must make the first move: "Ask, and it shall
be given you; seek, and you shall find; knock, and it shall be
opened unto you."[10] Infinite Intelligence, which is another name
for Isaiah's God, is ever ready to carry out our demands, whether
small or great.

Every desire, uttered or unexpressed, is a demand, but we're often startled by having a wish suddenly fulfilled. This happened to me once, in a beautiful way.

One Easter, having seen many beautiful rose trees in the florist's windows, I wished I would receive one and, for an instant, saw it in my mind's eye being carried in the door. Easter came and, with it, a beautiful rose tree. I thanked my friend the following day and told her it was just what I had wanted. She replied, "I didn't send you a rose tree. I sent you lilies!" The florist had mixed up the order, sending me a rose tree simply because I had started the law in action, and I had to have a rose tree.

The Power of Words

In about 600 BCE, the Buddha is reported to have said, "Words have the power to both destroy and heal. When words are both true and kind, they can change our world." "Death and Life are in the power of the tongue," says the ancient Hebrew proverb. Clearly, anyone who doesn't know the power of their words is way behind the times!

Many people have brought disaster into their lives through idle words. We need to remember that the subconscious mind is like a computer; it takes everything we say literally and has no sense of humor. Not knowing this, people often joke themselves into unhappy experiences.

A woman once asked me why her life was now one of poverty and limitation. She had previously had a home, had been surrounded by beautiful things, and had plenty of money. As we talked, we found she had often tired of the management of her home and had said repeatedly, "I'm sick and tired of things—

I wish I lived in a trunk," and she added, "Today I am living in that trunk." She had spoken herself into a trunk.

Another woman who had a great deal of money joked continually about "getting ready for the poorhouse." In a few years she was almost destitute, having impressed the subconscious mind with a picture of lack and limitation.

Fortunately the principle works both ways, and a situation of lack may be changed to one of plenty. Using the power of the spoken word, we can turn it around.

A woman came to me one hot summer's day for a treatment for prosperity. She was worn out, dejected, and discouraged. She said she possessed just eight dollars in the world. Since we taught that everyone has the power to bless and to multiply, to heal and to prosper, I said, "Good, we'll bless the eight dollars and multiply them as Jesus Christ multiplied the loaves and fishes."

She said, "What shall I do next?" I replied, "Follow your intuition. Do you have a hunch to do anything, or to go anywhere?" (Intuition means "in tuition," or to be taught from within. It's our unerring guide and will be dealt with more fully in chapter 8.)

The woman replied, "I don't know. I seem to have a hunch to go home; I've just enough money for carfare." Her home was in a distant city and was one of lack and limitation, and the reasoning mind (intellect) would have said, "Stay in New York and get work and make some money."

I replied, "Then go home; never violate a hunch." I spoke the following words for her: "Infinite Spirit, open the way for great abundance for _____. She is an irresistible magnet for all that belongs to her by divine right." I told her to repeat these words continually. She left for home immediately.

In calling on a woman near her home one day soon after, she connected with an old friend of her family's. Through this friend, she received thousands of dollars in a most miraculous way. She has often said to me since, "Tell people about the woman who came to you with eight dollars and a hunch."

We always have a silent listener at our side—our subconscious mind. Every thought, every word is impressed upon it like a singer recording a song; every note and tone of the singer's voice is registered, and if she coughs or hesitates, that is registered also.

It's time to erase all the old recordings stored in the subconscious mind. They're programs that the computer of our subconscious carries out in amazing detail, but they no longer serve us. So let's delete those we no longer wish to keep, and make new and beautiful programs for the future.

The chapters that follow will deal with the different methods of impressing the subconscious mind. It's our faithful servant, but we must be careful to give it the right orders!

Fear—The Only Block

A very brilliant man who has attained great success told me he had suddenly erased all fear from his consciousness by reading a sign that hung in a room he was visiting. He saw, printed in large letters, "Why worry? It will probably never happen." These words were stamped indelibly upon his subconscious mind, and he now has a firm conviction that only good can come into his life. Therefore, only good can manifest in his life.

Nothing stands between us and the experience of our heart's desires and highest ideals except doubt and fear. When we can wish without worrying, when we can expect without conflicting ideas, every desire of our hearts must be (meaning can't not be) instantly fulfilled.

As Franklin D. Roosevelt so clearly explained, fear is our only enemy. Fear of lack, fear of failure, fear of sickness, fear of loss, or feelings of insecurity—these are all that keep us from fulfilling our potential and having what is truly ours.

And as we understand this, we can see that we must learn to substitute faith for fear.

This is much easier to do when we realize that fear is only inverted faith—it's faith in what we don't want to have happen instead of what we want to happen. For example, when you set off on a trip afraid that your car will break down or traffic will cause delays, that's the same kind of faith as when you set off knowing that you'll easily arrive at your destination. We need the faith that we have when we reach to turn on a light: a sure knowledge, without any conflicting thought, that our action will bring us what we intend it to.

The next chapter will explain more fully the scientific reason for this and how fear can be erased from both the subconscious and conscious mind.

Summary

The first objective of the Game of Life is to clearly see your own good and to obliterate all mental pictures of distress or disease. This must be done by programming the subconscious mind with the realization that our goal is our full experience of the divine qualities of Health, Wealth, Love, and Perfect Self-Expression. These are the four aspects of being that make up the square of life that was the mystical goal of the ancient philosophers—they sought to "square the circle," to bring the material cycles of life

into spiritual perfection. With the fulfillment of these four qualities, the Game of Life is completed.

ESSENTIAL POINTS

- Our ability to create and see images in our minds plays a
leading part in how the Game of Life unfolds.
- Our own unique, perfect pattern is within each of us, and
when we focus on experiencing that more fully, all of life's
gifts manifest effortlessly and joyfully.
- The Principle of Substitution states that when the right idea
is substituted for a wrong one, there is no loss or sacrifice
involved.
- What we seek can only be brought into our experience
through our clear intention, our understanding of faith, and
the spoken word.
- The subconscious mind is like a computer: it takes everything
literally and has no sense of humor. As a result it's often filled
with programs that do not serve us.
- We need to delete the programs that we no longer wish to
keep and make new, beautiful programs for the future, which
are based on Spiritual Principles.
- Nothing stands between us and the attainment of our highest
ideals and the desires of our heart except our own doubt and
fear—which is only inverted faith.
- Health, Wealth, Love, and Perfect Self-Expression are the four
aspects of being that make up the square of life; they are the
Game completed.

EXERCISE

Researchers have established that our habits of thought and feeling
are related to patterns of connections between the cells of our
brains, and that these neural pathways can be disconnected and

reconnected over a period of twenty-eight days.[11] So every morn-ing and evening for twenty-eight days, speak these words aloud several times, until you can do so with power and conviction:

> *By my spoken word, I now delete and erase every untrue belief and program in my subconscious mind. They came from what others told me, combined with my own imaginings, and are dispersed into the nothingness from which they emerged. I now make new, perfect programs through the power of my true nature: programs to create Health, Wealth, Love, and Perfect Self-Expression.*

2

THE PRINCIPLE OF PROSPERITY

One of the greatest messages given to humanity through the many world scriptures is that all the resources we need for our fulfillment are always present, and that we can manifest through our spoken word all that belongs to us as our inherent birthright. The Spiritual Principle of perfect faith in our spoken word allows us to complete this part of the Game of Life. As the Sufi sage Rumi tells us, "You must ask for what you want."

Materialist scientists are now beginning to prove what metaphysicians have known for millennia: words and thoughts are a tremendous vibratory force, constantly shaping our bodies and environment, as well as our minds and relationships. The Buddha said, "We must be careful of our words." The Hebrew prophet Isaiah said, "My word shall not return unto me void, but shall accomplish that which it is sent to do."

This is the Principle we rely on in spiritual mind treatments: our word, spoken clearly and without conflicting thoughts or feelings, must always accomplish what we intend. This is what we must have faith in.

A woman came to me in great distress and said she was going to be sued on the fifteenth of the month for three thousand dollars. She knew of no way to get the money and was in despair. I told her God, the Source of all that is, was her supply and that there is a supply for every demand.

So I spoke the word. I gave thanks that the woman would receive three thousand dollars at the right time, in the right way. I told her she must have perfect faith and act her perfect faith.

The fifteenth came but no money had materialized. She called me on the phone and asked what to do. I replied, "It is Saturday, so they won't sue you today. Your part is to act rich, thereby showing perfect faith that you will receive it by Monday." She asked me to lunch with her to keep up her courage. When I joined her at a restaurant, I said, "This is no time to economize. Order an expensive luncheon and act as if you had already received the three thousand dollars."

The next morning she called me on the phone and asked me to stay with her during the day, I said, "No, you are divinely protected and Infinite Intelligence is never too late."

That evening she phoned again, greatly excited, and said, "My dear, a miracle has happened! I was sitting in my room this morning when the doorbell rang. I said to the maid, 'Don't let anyone in.' The maid, however, looked out the window and said, 'It's your cousin with the long white beard.'

"So I said, 'Call him back. I would like to see him.' He was just turning the corner when he heard the maid's voice, and he came back. We talked for about an hour, and just as he was leaving, he said, 'Oh, by the way, how are finances?' I told him I needed money, and he said, 'Why, my dear, I will give you three thousand dollars the first of the month.'

"I didn't want to tell him I was going to be sued. What shall I do? I won't receive it till the first of the month, and I must have it tomorrow."

I said, "I'll keep on treating. Spirit is never too late." I gave thanks she had received the money on the invisible plane and that it manifested on time.

The next morning, Monday, the first day of business after the fifteenth, her cousin called her up and said, "Come to my office this morning and I will give you the money." That afternoon, she had three thousand dollars to her credit in the bank and wrote checks as rapidly as her excitement would permit.

Our word never comes back unfulfilled.

Ask Believing

If we ask for success and yet prepare for failure, we'll get what we've prepared for.

A man came to me asking me to speak the word that a certain debt would be wiped out. He spent our time planning what he would say to the man when he did not pay his bill, thereby neutralizing my words. He should have seen himself paying the debt.

We have a wonderful illustration of this in the Hebrew Bible as well. When the kings of Israel were in the desert without water for their men and horses, they consulted the prophet Elisha, who gave them this astonishing message: "Thus says the Lord: You shall not see wind, neither shall you see rain, yet make this valley full of ditches." Accepting his authority as a prophet, they dug irrigation ditches in the dry desert land and were delighted when those same ditches were soon filled with flowing water.

We must prepare for the thing we've asked for—even, and especially, when there isn't the slightest sign of it in sight. Albert Einstein understood this principle when he wrote a letter of concern about the United States government's actions following World War II, saying, "You cannot simultaneously prepare for and prevent war."

The Principle can clearly be seen working in many people's lives.

> One woman found it necessary to look for an apartment during a year when there was a great shortage of apartments in New York. It was considered almost impossible, and her friends were sorry for her and said, "Isn't it too bad you'll have to store your furniture and live in a hotel." She replied, "You needn't feel sorry for me. I'm a superman, and I'll get an apartment." She spoke the words, until they were real to her: "Infinite Spirit, open the way for the right apartment."

The woman knew there was a supply for every demand, that she was not limited by material conditions because she was working on the spiritual plane, and that, as Wendell Phillips said, "One with God is a majority."[1]

> She had contemplated buying new blankets when the "tempter," the adverse thought or reasoning mind, suggested, "Don't buy the blankets. Perhaps, after all, you won't get an apartment and you will have no use for them." She promptly replied (to herself): "I'll dig my ditches by buying the blankets!" So she prepared for the apartment and acted as though she already had it.

She found her apartment in a miraculous way, and it was given to her although there were over two hundred other applicants. Buying the blankets showed her active faith.

We need to prepare for that which we want as if we expect it to happen. Then we will have our fulfillment, just as the ditches dug by the kings in the desert were eventually filled to overflowing.

Armies of Demons: Tormenting Thoughts

Getting into the spiritual swing of things is no easy matter. Very soon after we start, all our doubts and fears surge from the subconscious to distract us and turn us away from our goal.

Buddhist tradition tells us that when Gautama sat under the Bodhi tree, he knew that the life of delights he'd grown up in was not his true path and that the life of deprivation and self-torture he had chosen in reaction wasn't useful either. Then a young girl showed up with a bowl of his favorite rice pudding. It was the first real food he'd had in years, and with the first bite he experienced total satisfaction and realized how suffering could be ended for all time. He decided to sit under that tree until he knew how to share this realization with the world. Almost immediately, Mara, the lord of darkness, chaos, and materiality, attacked Gautama with all his armies—but the spears and arrows they shot at him became flowers as they landed around the unimpressed Gautama. The fearful images of what might be, the many temptations to fear, had no power over him; he put them to flight by dismissal, also called noninvolvement. Gautama made no effort to fight the apparent demons and so became the Buddha.

Similarly, Jesus, when tempted in the desert, simply turned away from earthly power and riches and so became the Christ.

In the modern world, Mohandas Gandhi avoided engaging the British in battle, but encouraged Indians to live—and do things the British had prohibited in order to take care of themselves—as if there were no British in control. By doing so, he freed India from the British Empire with minimal bloodshed, becoming a *Mahatma* (Great Soul, saint) in the process. Decades later, Martin Luther King Jr. used many of the same methods to end racial segregation and achieve racial equality in the United States.

Seeing, Dismissing, and Receiving

We can only receive what we see and feel ourselves receiving. In the Torah, the descendants of Israel were told that they could have all the land that they could see. This is true for everyone. We all have all the land within our own mental vision—but it's important to remember that we *only* have the land within that vision.

Expanding our vision is usually accompanied by tormenting thoughts. When we've made a statement of high spiritual truth, the old beliefs in the subconscious are challenged, and what the old metaphysicians called *error thought* is exposed, so it can be put out. This explains why it's so often darkest before the dawn.

In the Torah, when the Israelites finally reached the Promised Land, they were afraid to go in. "There we saw the giants and we were in our own sight as grasshoppers,"[2] they said. This is almost everyone's experience; our old programs tell us to fear the unknown, to see the new as strange and dangerous.

However, like Gautama under the Bodhi tree, the one who knows this Spiritual Principle is undisturbed by appearances. Such beings rejoice even while appearances suggest that they're "yet in captivity," and so are released—as the Hebrew prophets often encouraged and the New Testament apostles discovered.[3]

Every great work, every major accomplishment has been brought into manifestation through the act of holding to a vision and not being disturbed by appearances to the contrary. Like Peter, John, and Paul imprisoned or Jesus calling forth the entombed Lazarus, as described in the New Testament,[4] we must hold to our vision and give thanks that the end is accomplished, that we have already received. Then, whatever the block has been, it's removed and we are free to go on with our lives—and to the next level in the Game.

Often, though, just before the big achievement, come apparent failure and discouragement—our old world comes unglued as a new one, based on our new beliefs and vision, comes in to take its place. This is the time when we must make our affirmations repeatedly, and rejoice and give thanks that we have already received, that our gift is present, awaiting our recognition.

We all have the capacity to see an unheard-of end product, even when the rest of the world thinks it's impossible. Steve Jobs did it with Apple, and most entrepreneurs have to go through the process when they enter new technological or cultural territory. In the New Testament, Jesus says to the disciples, "Don't people say 'there are yet four months and then cometh the harvest'? Behold, I say unto you, lift up your eyes and look on the fields; for they are already ripe to harvest." His clear vision pierced the world of matter, and dismissing the lower-vibration appearances, he clearly saw the higher-vibration world—things as they really are—perfect and complete in the One, the ground of being, what Plato called the Divine Design.

Where Two or More Are Gathered

Sometimes a person may be too close to the circumstances, or becomes doubtful and fearful, and so may not be able to sustain the clarity of mind necessary to demonstrate results. Fortunately, however, a second person can remember and hold the truth of a situation. This is one of the reasons that Buddhists form spiritual communities, or *sanghas*. Jesus said, "If two of you shall agree on earth as touching anything that they shall ask, it shall be done for them."[5] This is why we turn to mental health practitioners and teachers to help us treat a situation and why many practitioners of mind treatment have someone treating them even as they treat their clients.

When we forget that appearances don't matter, we can sometimes stubbornly decide that what we intend is impossible. That's when we need to call on someone else to remind us of Truth.

A business owner came to me asking for treatments for success. It was imperative that he raise fifty thousand dollars for his business within a certain time. The time limit was almost up when he came to me in despair. No one wanted to invest in his enterprise, and the bank had flatly refused a loan.

I replied, "I suppose you lost your temper while at the bank, and therefore your power. You can control any situation if you first control yourself. Go back to the bank, and I will treat." My treatment was: "You are identified in love with the spirit of everyone connected with the bank. Let the divine idea come out of this situation."

He said, "Woman, you are talking about an impossibility. Tomorrow is Saturday; the bank closes at twelve, my train won't get me there until ten, and the time limit is up tomorrow, and anyway they won't do it. It's too late."

I replied, "Our Source doesn't need any time and is never too late. In divine timing all things are possible." I added, "I don't know anything about business, but I know all about God."

He replied, "It all sounds fine when I sit here listening to you, but when I go out it's terrible."

He lived in a distant city, and I didn't hear from him for a week; then came a letter. It read: "You were right. I raised the money and will never again doubt the truth of all that you told me."

I saw him a few weeks later, and I said, "What happened? You evidently had plenty of time after all."

He replied, "My train was late, and I got there just fifteen minutes to twelve. I walked into the bank and quietly said, 'I have come for the loan,' and they gave it to me without a question."

It was the last fifteen minutes of the time allotted to him, but Infinite Spirit is never too late. In this instance, he could never have demonstrated his desired results alone. He needed someone to help him hold the vision. This is what one person can do for another.

Someone else who understands these principles can clearly see the success, health, or prosperity we seek when we can't. And that other person never wavers because she/he is not too close to the situation. It's much easier to treat and experience demonstrations for someone else than for one's self, so none of us need hesitate to ask for help if our faith wavers, if we lose our knowledge that our heart's desires are fulfilled.

A keen observer of life once told me, "No one can fail if even one person sees us successful." Such is the power of true vision, and many great people have owed their success to a family member or a friend who believed in them and held to the perfect pattern without wavering.

Summary

To accomplish our destiny, we must always hold the vision of completing the Game, continuously demanding the immediate experience of all that we've already received in our mind. It may be our perfect health, love, supply, self-expression, home, or friends. It may be freedom from any form of distress. They're all finished and perfect ideas, registered in our own superconscious mind, which some call the Divine Mind.

However, they must come *through* our awareness—they never come to us. As we dismiss all distressing appearances as unreal, and become clear channels for the higher vibrating energy of the superconscious to flow through us to others, that energy brings the perfect experience into a form that fulfills our heart's desire.

ESSENTIAL POINTS

- Our supply is always present and we can reveal all that belongs to us as our inalienable birthright through our spoken word.

- If we ask for success and prepare for failure, we'll get what we have prepared for. Therefore we must prepare for the thing we've asked for, most especially when there isn't the slightest sign of it in sight.

- The fearful images of what might be, the many temptations to fear, must be put to flight by dismissal or noninvolvement.

- The one who knows this Spiritual Principle is undisturbed by appearances—we can hold to our vision and give thanks that the end is accomplished, that we've already received.

- One person is typically too close to his or her own circumstances and too often becomes doubtful and fearful, but a second person can remember and hold the truth of the situation.

- We continue to hold the vision of winning our Game, and demand the manifestation of all that we have already received in mind coming through to our awareness, as we dismiss all distressing or conflicting appearances.

EXERCISE

Think of something relatively unimportant that you would like to experience. It may be a particular food or a phone call from someone you haven't heard from or some small, new object in your life—whatever you would enjoy but doesn't have a whole lot of energy behind it.

Write it down as a statement in the present tense (we call that an affirmation) on a sticky note and stick it on the page for the next month on your calendar: "I now have (or am experiencing) _____."

Imagine what it would feel like and look like, even sound like or taste like, to experience this. Feel the delight, the pleasure, and the joy of having the experience and knowing that you have made it happen. Notice what thoughts come up and dismiss any thoughts that seem to say it's not possible or okay to experience it. If these doubts won't go away, write them down and cross them off, dismissing them as you do so, and rewrite your affirmation on a new sheet. Then tear up and burn the sheet of paper with all the dismissed doubts.

Now go about whatever you would normally be doing, giving no more thought to the experience you're intending.

As you're going on with your life, an opportunity may come up to do something as if you've already received the object or experience (as did the woman who bought the blankets in the story on page 20). If so, act as if you already have it, because in Truth, you do or this opportunity wouldn't have entered your awareness. Then, again, go about whatever you would normally be doing, giving no more thought to the experience you're intending.

As the next month comes along, check the sticky note. If it's happened, congratulate yourself! You've made it through another level in the Game of Life and opened the door to a whole new world of possibilities! If it has not yet happened, move it to the following month and make sure you haven't been preparing for failure. If you have been, stop doing those things. Again, dismiss any thoughts that seem to say it's not possible or okay to experience it. If they won't go away, write them down and cross them off, dismissing them as you do so, and rewrite your affirmation. Then tear up the sheet of paper.

Repeat the above until the intended experience—or something even better!—has happened.

3

The Power of Words

Through our spoken word, we're continually making laws for ourselves—we're programming our subconscious mind to shape and attract substance, people, and events to support our words. This principle can work in our favor—or against us—but it is always working.

> *I knew a man who said, "I always miss cabs. They invariably pull out just as I arrive." His daughter said, "I always catch cabs. They're sure to come just as I get there." They continued to have this experience for years. They had made different laws for their lives: one of failure, one of success.*

Once we know the power of the spoken word, we become very careful in our conversations. We only have to watch the world's reaction to our words to know that they always accomplish something. Jesus taught this principle, saying, "By your words you shall be acquitted, and by your words shall you be condemned."[1]

Superstitious Beliefs

The power of our spoken word explains the psychology of superstitions. The horseshoe or rabbit's foot contains no power in itself, but our words and belief that it will bring us good luck create a program of expectancy in the subconscious mind, which then attracts and encourages us to see a lucky situation.

I find, however, this no longer works when someone has advanced spiritually and knows a higher law. As was promised to the Israelites on Mount Sinai and to Mohammed in the cave above Mecca, once we've experienced the one, universal Power and Presence, we can't turn back; we must put away the "graven images" or "false idols" that we've created by expecting an object, a job, or a relative to answer our prayer for fulfillment.

> *For example: Two men in my class had had great success in business for several months when suddenly everything went to smash. We tried to analyze the situation, and I found that, instead of making their affirmations and looking to the divine for success and prosperity, they had each bought a lucky monkey.*
>
> *I said: "Oh, I see, you have been trusting in the lucky monkeys instead of the Source." I told them, "Put away the lucky monkeys and call on the Principle of Forgiveness," for we all have the power to forgive or neutralize our mistakes.*
>
> *They decided to throw the lucky monkeys into the fire and all went well again.*

This does not mean that we should throw away every lucky ornament or horseshoe around the house; it does mean, instead, that we must recognize that the power behind such things is the one and only Power. As the Qur'an reminds us, "There is no god

but Allah,"[2] and no object has any power beyond simply reminding us of that Power.

*A friend of mine demonstrated this difference beautifully. One
day she was in deep despair. While crossing the street, she picked
up a horseshoe. Immediately she was filled with joy and hope.
She said God had sent her the horseshoe in order to keep up her
courage. It was, at that moment, about the only thing that could
have registered in her consciousness. Her hope became faith, and
she ultimately made a wonderful demonstration of good.*

I wish to make the point clear that the men previously mentioned were depending on the monkeys alone while this woman
recognized a higher power behind the horseshoe.

I know in my own case, it took a long while to get out of a
belief that a certain thing brought disappointment. If that thing happened, disappointment invariably followed. I found that the only
way I could make a change in the subconscious was by asserting the
following: "There are not two powers; there is only one power,
which we call God. The One Power is only for good; therefore,
there are no disappointments and this thing means a happy surprise."
This became my continual affirmation. I noticed a change at once,
and happy surprises commenced coming my way.

*Not everyone finds their statement easily though. I have a friend
who said that nothing could induce her to walk under a ladder.
I said, "If you are afraid, you are giving in to a belief in two
powers, Good and Evil, instead of one. As God is absolute, there
can be no opposing power, unless someone makes up a false
power of evil for himself. To show you believe in only One
Power, the Divine Good, and that there is no power or reality in
evil, walk under the next ladder you see."*

Soon after, she went to her bank. She wished to open her safety-deposit box, but there stood a ladder in her way. It was impossible to reach the box without passing under the ladder. She cowered with fear and turned back. She could not face the lion on her path. However, when she reached the street, my words rang in her ears and she decided to return and walk under it. It was a big moment in her life, for ladders had held her in bondage for years. She retraced her steps to the vault, and the ladder was no longer there!

This often happens. If we're willing to do something we are afraid to do, we often find that we no longer have to. This is the Principle of Nonresistance, which is little understood but which all can benefit from. (It will be addressed in some detail in chapter 4.)

A popular saying tells us that courage contains genius and magic.[3] Face a situation fearlessly and "magically" there's no longer a situation to face; it falls away of its own weight. Fear attracted the ladder on the woman's pathway and fearlessness removed it.

Our Words Create and Attract Our Experience

The invisible forces are always working and we're always pulling the strings, though we generally don't even know that we're doing it. Because of the vibratory power of words, whatever anyone voices, they begin to attract. As everyone in nursing school or medical school discovers, people who continually speak of disease invariably experience it.

Once we know how things work, we can't be too careful of our words. For example, I have a friend who often says on the phone,

"Come to see me and have a nice old-fashioned chat." This "old-fashioned chat" means an hour of about five hundred to a thousand destructive words, the principal topics being loss, lack, failure, and sickness.

I reply, "No, thank you. I've had enough 'old-fashioned chats' in my life; they are too expensive, but I will be glad to have a new-fashioned chat and talk about what we want, not what we don't want."

There's an old saying: "A man only dares use his words for three purposes: to heal, bless, or prosper."

Remember, the Game of Life is a game of receiving what we give. If we wish to help someone succeed, we're wishing and helping ourselves to succeed as well; if someone wishes someone bad luck, that person is sure to attract bad luck himself. What someone says of others will be said of him, and what we wish for another, we are wishing for ourselves. Or to use a more homely metaphor, "Curses, like chickens, come home to roost."

Healing Words

Illness is another condition that our words affect. The metaphysician knows that all disease has a mental equivalent, and in order to heal the body, one must first heal the soul. The soul is the subconscious mind, and wrong programs recorded in the past must be erased if it is to attract the circumstances and resources for a healthy body.

As Louise Hay has helped the world understand, every disease is caused by a mind not at ease.[4] Continual criticism produces rheumatism because critical, inharmonious thoughts cause unnatural deposits in the blood, which settle in the joints. False growths (which may be diagnosed as tumors, cysts, or cancers) are caused by jealousy, hatred, unforgivingness, fear, and so on. I said once in my class, "There is no use asking someone 'What is the matter with you?' We might more effectively say, '*Who* is the matter with you?'" Unforgivingness is the most prolific cause of disease. It will harden arteries, destroy the liver, and affect the eyesight.

Endless forms of illness result from this all-too-human tendency, including symptoms that appear to have been caused by something that bit us or that we've eaten.

I called on a woman one day, who said she was ill from having eaten a poisoned oyster. I replied, "Oh, no, the oyster was harmless; you poisoned the oyster. Who's the matter with you?" She answered, "Oh, about nineteen people." She had quarreled with nineteen people and had become so inharmonious that she attracted the wrong oyster.

Psalm 23 of the Hebrew Bible says, "He restoreth my soul." This means that the subconscious mind is restored with the right ideas so that the conscious mind and body may be healthy.

In the world's indigenous cultures and the ancient mystery schools that maintained the spiritual remnants of those cultures, the *heiros gamos*, or "mystical marriage," was practiced as a form of this healing process. While it was outwardly celebrated by a man and a woman to bring harmony to the community, according to the inner, esoteric teachings, the *heiros gamos* is the marriage of the soul and the spirit, which we would call the union of the subconscious and superconscious mind. They must be one if we are to complete the many levels of the Game of Life—and in truth, the Game exists to help us achieve the union of these two aspects of being.

In the Christian tradition, when both the conscious and subconscious minds are flooded with the perfect ideas of the superconscious, it's said that "I and the Father are one." In other words, we, as the emanations of the divine, become one with the realm of perfect ideas. As spiritual traditions around the world agree, we are the divine likeness and image, and as such we are given power and dominion over all created things: our mind, our body, and our circumstances. Experiencing the divine union means that we do so divinely—that is to say, in accordance with the divine pattern that is, as Plato discovered, embedded in our superconscious mind.

In that mystical union, through the spoken word and clear vision, the body may be renewed and transformed, continuous abundant supply may be established, and disease can be completely wiped out of the consciousness. This means that all conscious experience, past and present, near and far, is freed of dis-ease—so the world around us is made whole as we heal ourselves!

Words of Love and Goodwill

It's safe to say that all sickness and unhappiness come from violations of the Principle of Love. This planet is being initiated in love, and the tendency to put down or control others is one of the last enemies to be overcome. The Buddha encouraged a compassionate heart. Jesus said, "A new commandment I give unto you: 'Love one another,'"[5] and in the Game of Life, love and compassion, which may also be called goodwill, take us through every level.

A woman I know had a terrible skin disease for years. The doctors told her it was incurable, and she was in despair. She worked in theater, and she feared she would soon have to give up her profession when she had no other means of support. Then she found a good gig and, on the opening night, was a great hit. The critics were flattering and she was elated.

The next day she received notice she'd been dismissed. Someone in the cast had been jealous of her success and had gotten her fired. She felt hatred and resentment taking complete possession of her, and she cried out, "Oh God, don't let me hate that man." That night she worked for hours, holding that intention.

She said, "I soon came into a very deep silence. I seemed to be at peace with myself, with the man, and with the whole world. I continued this for two more nights, and on the third day, I found I was healed completely of the skin disease!"

In asking for love, or at least goodwill, she had fulfilled the law (as Paul tells us, "for love is the fulfilling of the law"), and the disease (which came from her subconscious resentment) was wiped out.

Any disharmony in our external situation is a clue, an indicator, that there is mental disharmony. The great metaphysician of the ancients, Hermes Trismegistus, is often quoted as saying, "As within, so without." He's telling us that what we see outside ourselves, in our bodies and in the world around us, is showing us what's going on inside our subconscious mind. The Sufi poet Rumi said, in about 1250 CE, "To praise the sun is to praise your own eyes." And in modern twelve-step programs, the phrase is: "If you spot it, you got it."

In the New Testament we're told "And a man's foes shall be they of his own household."[6] This is a metaphor reminding people to look within for the source of their problems. Our only enemies are within our own minds, and they can best be dealt with there.

The fundamental laws of Judaism and Christianity are sometimes called the "two-law," which, in both bibles, is "Love God with all your heart, mind, and soul, and love your neighbor as yourself."[7] And their message is "Peace on Earth, goodwill toward mankind." In the New Testament verses known as the Beatitudes, we're told "Love your enemies, bless them that curse you, do good to them that hate you, and pray for them which spitefully use you and persecute you."[8] This means that our work is within ourselves; we need to realize that when others' behavior toward us is unloving, it simply shows us our own lack of love, so we are to send out goodwill and blessings to everyone.

All spiritual traditions express very much the same message and law. It's the Principle of Love. Those who become enlightened are therefore actually perfecting themselves through their relationships with their neighbors and family members.

As the Hebrew prophet Isaiah said, the marvelous thing is, when we are filled with goodwill, "No weapon that is formed against you shall prosper."[9] That is, if we bless someone, they have no power to harm us!

Someone came to me asking to treat for success in business. He was selling machinery and a rival had appeared on the scene with what he proclaimed was a better machine. My friend feared defeat.

I said, "First of all, we must wipe out all fear and know that the universe is a perfect design, protecting your well-being, and that the divine idea must come out of the situation. That is, the right machine will be sold by the right man to the right man." And I added, "Don't hold one critical thought toward that man. Bless him all day and be willing not to sell your machine if it isn't the divine idea."

So he went to his meetings fearless and nonresistant and blessing the other man. In reporting the results to me later, my friend said that the outcome was remarkable. The other man's machine refused to work, so he sold his without the slightest difficulty.

This is how the Principle of Love works, changing our inner and outer experience at the same time.

Summary

Goodwill produces an aura of well-being around those who send it. This is why the great masters of so many traditions have sent their disciples into the world with few belongings and no physical protection. They knew that love and goodwill destroy the dissonant thoughts and feelings within one's self, so there's no internal disharmony. As a result we have no disease in the body and nothing outside us to be protected from.

ESSENTIAL POINTS

- Through our spoken word, we're programming our subconscious mind to shape and attract substance, people, and events.
- The horseshoe or rabbit's foot contains no power, but our spoken word and the belief that it will bring us good luck create a program of expectancy in the subconscious mind.
- There are not two powers; there is only one, all-powerful, which is the meaning of Omnipotent. The One Power is only for good; therefore, there is no power of evil in the world and no disappointments are real.
- Face a situation fearlessly and there is no longer a situation to face; it falls away of its own weight. This is the Principle of Nonresistance.
- "A man only dares use his words for three purposes: to heal, bless or prosper." If we wish to help someone succeed, we're helping ourselves succeed as well.
- All disease has a mental equivalent, and in order to heal the body, one must first heal the soul, or subconscious mind,

from wrong programs recorded in the past. Then, through the spoken word and clear vision, the body may be renewed and transformed and disease can be completely wiped out of the consciousness.

- "As within, so without." Any disharmony in our external situation is a clue, an indicator that there is mental disharmony. Our only enemies are within ourselves. This is the Principle of Reflection.

- Love and goodwill destroy the enemies within one's self so there is no internal disharmony; then we have no disease in the body and no external enemies. This is the Principle of Love.

EXERCISE

As you look over your life and health, you may find aspects that aren't as whole and perfect as you'd like them to be.

If there's any disease or disharmony in your life, don't ask, "What's the matter with me?" Instead ask, "*Who* is the matter with me?" Make a list of all the people who come to mind when you ask that question. They may be people you're angry at or afraid of, people you think are doing things that are harmful, or people you resent or feel have hurt you in some way—either directly or indirectly—through their words or actions.

Look one at a time at the names you've written. Imagine each person, and in your mind untie the cords that have bound you to them, releasing both of you. Then bless them on their way, *feeling* sure that all is well with them and with you.

When you've completed your list, shred it or burn it, saying something like, "I release you and let you go, giving thanks for the gift you have been in my life."

If any negative feelings come up toward any of these people during this process, let yourself feel those feelings; you can even write them down, then tear up that piece of paper or burn it.

Then go find a rock or something that symbolizes the feelings you've had and throw it as far as you safely can—into the ocean or a lake or river is wonderful—telling yourself, "I am done with this! I release this! It no longer has any effect on my thoughts or my life!" Then go back to your list of people and repeat the first part of the process.

4

THE PRINCIPLE OF NONRESISTANCE

Nothing on earth can resist an absolutely nonresistant person. The Tao Te Ching says that water is the most powerful element because it's perfectly nonresistant. It wears away rocks and sweeps all before it.

Evil as an Illusion in Collective Consciousness

There's an old legend in the Vedas that Adam and Eve ate of the tree of *maya* (illusion), and so saw two powers instead of the One Power, which we call God. This means that evil is a false law that someone has made up.

Jesus said, "Get thee behind me" when Peter started to express fears about his safety,[1] for Jesus knew that in reality there is no evil and therefore nothing to fear. He knew that the idea of evil is the result of humanity's "vain imagination" that we're separated from the ground of being that is our Source. This imagining resulted in a belief in two powers, good and evil, or more accurately, the presence and absence of good.

The New Thought "teacher of teachers," Emma Curtis Hopkins, says in her second lesson that since most of humanity believes our good is absent from us, that belief had to have a name and so was called evil. She goes on to say that the concept is empty, having no power, since God—as good—is omnipotent, meaning that no other power can exist.[2]

The false belief called evil is maintained across the generations through what some people call psychoma, or soul sleep. Soul sleep means that the subconscious mind has been hypnotized by the illusions (of such things as sin, sickness, and death) of the collective consciousness (also called carnal or mortal thought) and our circumstances are projections of our illusions in the world around us.

In the first chapter, it was explained that our soul is our subconscious mind and whatever we feel deeply, good or bad, is made manifest in our outer world by that faithful servant. Our bodies and circumstances reflect whatever we've been imagining. At some level, consciously or unconsciously, the sick person has imagined sickness; the poor person, poverty; the rich person, wealth. Those images, more than any circumstance, brought about their situation.

Too often those images come from the people around us. We tend to accept the ideas given to us by authority figures or advertisements as if they were, in fact, our own beliefs. We imagine what those ideas might lead to and then are surprised when we experience them. One Unity minister used to say to her congregation, "Watch out, now, the advertisers are starting to tell you that it's 'flu season' but it's really just time for you to tell them they have no control over you."

People often say, "Why does a little child attract illness when it's too young even to know what it means?" I answer that children are sensitive and receptive to the thoughts of others around them and often manifest the fears or expectations of their parents. (Emerson used to say that students will always learn what the teacher tries to hide from them.)[3] These parents unconsciously attract illness and disaster to their children by continually holding them in thoughts of fear and watching for symptoms. As an example, a friend asked a woman if her little girl had had the measles. She replied promptly, "Not yet!" implying that she was expecting the illness, therefore preparing the way for what she did not want for herself or her child.

I once heard a metaphysician say, "If you do not run your subconscious mind, someone else will run it for you."

Transmutation through Nonresistance

However, someone who is centered and established in right thinking, someone who sends out only goodwill to humanity and who is without fear, can't be touched or influenced by the negative thoughts of others. In fact, such people can receive only good thoughts, as they themselves send forth only good thoughts.

· A metaphysician who had once been a Christian minister gave me a wonderful recipe for completing every level in the Game of Life: *be the epitome of nonresistance*. He presented it this way: "At one time in my life, I baptized children, and of course, they had many names. Now I no longer baptize children, but I baptize events—and I give them all the same name. Even if I have a failure, I baptize it Success, in the name of the Father, the Son, and the Holy Ghost!" Now, we don't have to use his Christian language, but we, too, can reframe every situation as Success.

In this, we see the great Principle of Transmutation, founded on nonresistance. Through our spoken word every apparent failure is transmuted into Success.

Once a woman who required money was trying to practice the Spiritual Principle of Opulence. She knew that in order to demonstrate her supply, she must first feel that she had received, that a feeling of opulence must precede its manifestation. But she continually found herself in the presence of someone who made her feel very poor. He talked lack and limitation and she began to catch his poverty thoughts, so she disliked him and blamed him for her failure.

It dawned on her one day that she was resisting the situation and seeing two powers instead of one. So she blessed the man and baptized the situation "Success." She affirmed, "As there is only one power and it is Good, this person is here for my good and my prosperity," even though that was just what he had not seemed to be there for.

Soon after that, through this man, she met a woman who hired her for a job and paid her several thousand dollars for it. The man then moved to a distant city and faded harmoniously from her life.

A useful reminder is, "Bless your enemy and you rob him of his ammunition." As we've seen more than once in this text, if you bless anyone you fear may harm you, his arrows will be transmuted into blessings. If you make the statement "Everyone is a golden link in the chain of my good," you'll begin to find that all people are your good in manifestation, waiting for the opportunity to serve the Divine Plan of your life.

This law is true of nations as well as individuals. As we learned during the Marshall Plan and the final years of the Cold War, when we bless a nation, sending love and goodwill to every inhabitant, it's robbed of its power to harm.

Humanity can only grasp the right idea of nonresistance through spiritual understanding. My students have often said, "I don't want to be a doormat." I reply, "When you use nonresis-tance with wisdom, no one will ever be able to walk over you." This is the essence of the form of nonviolence that Gandhi used called *satyagraha*, by which he led the movement to convince the British to grant India its independence.

Gandhi said, "Satyagraha is a relentless search for truth and a determination to reach truth. It is a force that works silently and apparently slowly. In reality, there is no force in the world that is so direct or so swift in working."[4]

The practice is subtle. We have to be willing to experience what's unfolding while still insisting on the intended results and not letting any appearance contrary to those results affect us. My own experience may illustrate the distinction.

One day I was impatiently awaiting an important telephone call. I resisted every call that came in and made no outgoing calls myself, reasoning that it might interfere with the one I was awaiting.

Instead of saying, "Divine ideas never conflict. The call will come at the right time," and leaving it to Infinite Intelligence to arrange, I tried to manage things myself. I made the battle mine and remained tense and anxious for hours.

At one point I realized the phone hadn't rung for about an hour and I glanced down and found that the phone was discon-nected! My anxiety, fear, and belief in interference had brought on a total telephone breakdown. Realizing what I'd done, I immedi-ately began blessing the situation; I baptized it "success," and affirmed, "I cannot lose any call that belongs to me by divine right; I am under divine grace and not under material law."

Because the signal had been broken, it had to be reconnected at the phone company's exchange, so a friend rushed down the street to the nearest telephone to notify the telephone company to reconnect. She entered a grocery, and though it was crowded, the proprietor left his customers and attended to the call himself. My phone was reconnected at once, and I relaxed. Two minutes later, I received one very important call; then about an hour afterward, I received the one I had been waiting for.

All pain comes from resistance. Resistance is hell, for it creates a state of torment. So long as people resist a situation, it will have its way with them. If they run away from it, it will run after them.

I repeated this to a woman one day and she replied, "How true that is! I was unhappy at home. I disliked my mother, who was critical and domineering, so I ran away and was married—but I married my mother, for my husband was exactly like her, and I had the same situation to face again."

Jesus said, "Agree with your adversary quickly."[5] The Qur'an tells us, "The good deed and the evil deed are not alike. Repel the evil deed with one which is good then lo! he, between whom and thee there was enmity will become as though he was a bosom friend."[6]

This means that when we agree that the apparently adverse situation is, in fact, good and we're undisturbed by it, it falls away of its own weight. "None of these things move me" is a wonderful affirmation.

All inharmonious situations come from some disharmony within ourselves. When there's no more emotional response to an inharmonious situation, it fades away from our pathway forever.

Always Within

It's clear now that our work is always within our own self, never focused on others. People have said to me, "Give treatments to change someone else." And I reply, "No, I will give treatments to change you. When you change, other people will change."

This is the Principle of Reflection, and it was nicely illustrated by a situation with one of my students.

This student was in the habit of lying. I told her it was a method that would lead to failure and if she lied, she would be lied to. She replied, "I don't care. I can't possibly get along without lying."

One day she was speaking on the phone to someone with whom she was very much in love. She turned to me and said, "I don't trust him. I know he's lying to me." I replied, "Well, you lie yourself, so someone has to lie to you, and you may be sure it will be just the person you want the truth from." Sometime after that, I saw her, and she said, "I'm cured of lying."

I asked, "What cured you?"

She replied, "I've been living with a woman who lies worse than I did!"

Life is a mirror, and we find only ourselves reflected in the people around us, so we are often cured of our own faults by seeing them in others.

There Is No Past

Living in the past is also a method of failure and a violation of Spiritual Principle. In the Hebrew Bible, Lot's wife looked back and was turned into a pillar of salt. Jesus said, "Behold, now is the accepted time; behold, now is the day of salvation."[7]

The robbers of time are the past and the future. We should bless the past, forgetting it if it keeps us in bondage, and bless the future, knowing it has endless joys in store for us, while we live fully in the now.

> *A woman came to me complaining that she had no money with which to buy Christmas gifts. She said, "Last year was so different; I had plenty of money and gave lovely presents, and this year I have scarcely a cent."*
>
> *I replied, "You will never demonstrate money while you live in the past. Live fully in the now, and get ready to give Christmas presents. Dig your ditches, and the money will come."*
>
> *She exclaimed, "I know what to do! I will buy some tinsel, twine, Christmas stickers, and wrapping paper." I replied, "Do that and the presents will come and stick themselves to the Christmas stickers."*
>
> *This, too, was showing financial fearlessness and faith in God when the reasoning mind said, "Keep every cent you have, because you're not sure you'll get any more."*
>
> *She bought the stickers, paper, and twine, and a few days before Christmas, received a gift of several hundred dollars. Buying the stickers and twine had impressed the subconscious with expectancy and opened the way for the manifestation of the money. Then she joyfully purchased all the presents in plenty of time.*

Living Expectantly

To complete the Game of Life successfully, we must be spiritually alert, constantly watching for leads and signs and taking advantage of every opportunity. This means we must live in the moment. As the great Sanskrit poet Kalidasa said more than two thousand five hundred years ago, "Look well, therefore, to this day; such is the salutation of the dawn."

One day when I was seeking an opportunity, I said continually, silently, "Infinite Spirit, don't let me miss a single clue," and something very important was told to me that evening.

It's really important to begin each day with right words. Make this a habit and you'll see wonders and miracles come into your life. One morning I picked up a book and read, "Look with wonder at that which is before you!" It seemed to be my message for the day, so I repeated it again and again. Imagine my wonder and delight when, about noon, a large sum of money was given me, money that I had been wanting for a certain purpose.

At the end of this section, I'll list the affirmations that I've found most effective. They're very powerful tools for changing our habits of thought; however, we should never use an affirmation unless it is absolutely satisfying and convincing to our own consciousness. This means that often, when working with others, an affirmation must be changed to suit the different people we're working with.

This affirmation has brought success to many:

I do wonderful work in a wonderful way;
I give wonderful service for wonderful pay!

I gave the first line to one of my students and she added the last line. It made a powerful statement, since there should always be perfect payment for perfect service, and a rhyme sinks easily into the subconscious. She went about singing it aloud and soon received a great job in which she truly did wonderful work in a wonderful way and gave wonderful service for wonderful pay!

Another student, a businessman, took it and changed the word "work" to "business." For a whole morning he repeated, "I have a wonderful business in a wonderful way, and I give wonderful service for wonderful pay." That afternoon he made a forty-one-thousand-dollar deal, though there had been no activity in his business for months.

Every affirmation must be carefully worded to completely cover the ground of the issues being addressed. Not doing so has caused all sorts of difficulties.

I knew a woman who was in great need and demanded work in her affirmation. She received a great deal of work but was never paid anything. She now knows to add "wonderful service for wonderful pay."

Summary

It's our divine right to have plenty—more than enough! Our pantries should be full and our cups should overflow. This is the divine idea for all humanity; it's our birthright! We can claim it for ourselves, and as we go about our lives, resisting nothing but having all, we shall break down the barriers of belief in lack held in our collective consciousness. Realizing that we need to hang on to nothing (the Principle of Nonattachment) and not resist anyone or any process (the Principle of Nonresistance), we shall find ourselves effortlessly receiving all that is ours when we can best make use of it. Then the Golden Age will be ours, and every righteous desire of all hearts shall be fulfilled!

Essential Points
- In reality there is no evil and therefore nothing to resist.
- The subconscious mind has been hypnotized by the illusions (such as of sin, sickness, and death) of the collective con-

sciousness, and our circumstances are projections of our illusions onto the world around us.

- So long as we resist a situation, it will have its way with us. If we run away from it, it will run after us. When we agree that the adverse situation is good and are not disturbed by it, then it falls away.

- Life is a mirror, and we find only ourselves reflected in the people around us.

- When we are centered, sending out only goodwill to humanity, and are without fear, we cannot be touched or influenced by the negative thoughts of others. In fact, we can then receive only good thoughts, as we ourselves radiate only good thoughts.

- We all need to bless the past, forgetting it if it keeps us in bondage; bless the future, knowing it has endless joys in store for us; and live fully in the now, spiritually alert, waiting for our leads and taking advantage of every opportunity.

- Every affirmation must be carefully worded to completely cover the issues being addressed. Unless an affirmation is absolutely satisfying and convincing to our own consciousness, it will not work.

- It's our divine right to have plenty. More than enough. Our pantries should be full and our cups overflow; this is the perfect pattern for humanity.

EXERCISE

For the next twenty-eight days, as you're opening your eyes each morning, immediately upon waking, make an affirmation for the day that helps you stay in the now, open to the possibilities emerging in the perfect pattern of your superconscious mind. You can use one from this chapter or from the back of this section if nothing comes to mind. Another example that's proven to be powerful is this:

The divine good will be done this day! Today is a day of delightful completion and discovery! I give thanks for this perfect day. Miracle shall follow miracle and wonders shall never cease!

The goal is to cover the range of possibilities or issues that you're aware of, have it feel comfortable and fitting for you, and be able to say it several times with the deep feeling—conviction, even—that it is so.

5

KARMA AND THE PRINCIPLE OF FORGIVENESS

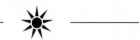

The Game of Life is a game of boomerangs: all our thoughts, deeds, and words return to us sooner or later, with astounding accuracy. We receive only what we give.

This is the Hindu and Buddhist law of Karma, which is Sanskrit for *action that has consequences*. In Christianity, it's stated as "Whatsoever you sow, that shall you also reap." In both traditions, the process may be conscious or unconscious. Krishna tells Arjuna in the Gita: "If a sincere person tries to control the active senses by the mind and begins the path of action without attachment, he is by far superior."[1]

A friend once said to me, "I make all my Karma with my aunt. Whatever I say to her, someone says to me. I am often irritable at home and one day said to my aunt, who was talking to me during dinner, 'No more talk, I wish to eat in peace.'

"The following day, I was lunching with a woman with whom I wished to make a great impression. I was talking animatedly when she said, 'No more talk, I wish to eat in peace!'"

My friend is a person who's very aware. She's focused on the spiritual more than the mental so is high in consciousness, and her Karma returns much more quickly to her than to someone who's focused on the mental; we might even say she has "instant Karma."

The more we know, the more we are responsible for, and someone with knowledge of the Spiritual Principle who doesn't practice it suffers greatly and immediately in consequence.

Yet we can be freed of Karma. In the Gita, Krishna, having already explained, "I am the birthless, the deathless, the Lord of all that breathes," tells the young prince Arjuna, "If your heart is united with me, you will be set free from karma even in this life."[2] Jesus on the cross taught forgiveness as the path of freedom, telling even convicted thieves that they would be with him that day in Paradise.[3]

Understanding Spiritual Principle

The Hebrew Bible tells us, "The fear of the Lord is the beginning of wisdom."[4] Sadly, though, this translation is both inaccurate and misleading. If we read the word "Lord" more accurately as "Universal Principle" and the word "fear" according to its root meaning of "single-eyed," many passages in the Torah, Qur'an, and the Old and New Testaments become much clearer. When we do so, for example, the above statement becomes: "Our single-eyed attention to Universal Principle is the beginning of wisdom."

This can be applied similarly with the Hebrew doctrine "I will repay, says the Lord." There are two aspects of the One Power: the transcendent, impersonal Principle that works regardless of person or context and the immanent, loving Presence felt by the spirit-focused individual. It's the Universal Principle that repays, not the loving Presence that Christians call "Our Father," whom Jesus called *Abwoon* ("loving, nurturing presence"), *Abba* ("daddy"), and "the Comforter." The transcendent Source simply Is; the immanent Presence shares our lives. Messianic Jews call the Presence *Emanuel*, Kabbalistic Jews call it *Shekinah*, Muslims call it *Allah*, many Buddhists call it *Tara*, most Hindus call it *Krishna*, Sufis often call it *The Beloved*, and Ralph Waldo Emerson called it *Over-Soul*.

This unconditionally loving Comforter sees only our perfection, sees humanity "created in our own image" with "power and dominion" over all other forms of being, as described in the first chapters of the book of Genesis.

The immanent Presence recognizes the perfect idea of humanity and is waiting patiently for our recognition because the nature of free will is such that we can only be what we see ourselves to be and only achieve what we see ourselves achieving. Jesus said, "And ye shall know the truth and the truth shall make you free."[5] He told us this so we might realize that freedom from all unhappy conditions comes through knowledge of Spiritual Principle. In the Bhagavad Gita, Krishna said, "When a man enters Reality...the recollected mind is awake in the knowledge of the Atman ... he knows peace ..."[6]

Desire is a tremendous force and must be directed in the right channels or chaos ensues. The Divine Pattern is the only safe pattern to work by. And, as with any form of power, we must understand and obey the principle before we can effectively use it. Electricity's principles must be obeyed before it becomes humanity's servant; when handled ignorantly, it becomes humanity's deadly foe, like nuclear power. So it is also with the laws of Mind! Obedience precedes authority, and the Principle obeys those who obey the Principle.

When working to bring a demonstration of Principle into material form, the most important step is the first step: to ask or claim properly. We should always demand only that which is ours by divine right. This is particularly well illustrated in the following example.

A woman with a strong personal will wished she owned a house that belonged to an acquaintance, and she often made mental pictures of herself living in the house. Over the course of time, the owner died and she moved into the house. Several years afterward, coming into the knowledge of Spiritual Principle, she said to me, "Do you think I had anything to do with that man's death?"

I replied, "Yes, your desire was so strong, everything made way for it, but you paid your Karmic debt. Your husband, whom you loved devotedly, died soon after, and the house was a white elephant for years."

The original owner, however, could not have been affected by her thoughts had he been positive in the truth, nor could her husband, but they were both unaware so lived under Karmic law.

Feeling such great desire for the house, the woman would have been happier had she said, "Infinite Intelligence, give me the right house, just as charming as this—the house which is mine by divine right." The One Power would have worked out everything to perfect satisfaction through the divine pattern and brought good to all. Had she taken the attitude "If the house I desire is mine, I cannot lose it; if it is not, give me its equivalent," the owner might have decided to move out harmoniously or another, even more desirable house would have been substituted. Anything forced into manifestation through personal will is always ill gotten and has bad results.

Across spiritual traditions, humanity is admonished, "My [the divine] will be done, not thine," and the curious thing is, we always get just what we truly desire when we relinquish personal will and enable Infinite Power and Intelligence to work through us. As Moses told the Israelites on the shore of the Sea of Reeds, "Stand still and see the salvation of the Lord [Universal Principle]."[7]

Learning to stand still seems so difficult for us! A woman came to me in great distress. Her daughter had determined to take a very hazardous trip, and the mother was filled with fear. She said she had used every argument, had pointed out the dangers to be encountered, and had forbidden her to go, but the daughter became more and more rebellious and determined.

I said to the mother, "You're forcing your personal will upon your daughter, which you have no right to do, and your fear of this trip is only attracting it, for you attract what you fear."

I added, "Let go, and take your mental hands off. Put the whole thing in the divine design, and use this statement: 'I put this situation in the hands of Infinite Love and Wisdom; if this trip is the divine plan, I bless it and no longer resist, but if it is not divinely planned, I give thanks that it is now dissolved and dissipated.'"

A day or two after that, her daughter said to her, "Mother, I've given up the trip," and the fear-filled situation returned to its native nothingness.

This Principle is developed further in the previous chapter on the Principle of Nonresistance.

Forgiveness

Another example of sowing and reaping came in the most curious way. A woman came to me saying she had received a counterfeit twenty-dollar bill from the bank. She was very concerned because, as she said, "The people at the bank will never acknowledge their mistake."

I replied, "Let us analyze the situation and find out why you attracted it." She thought a few moments and exclaimed, "I know—I sent a friend a lot of stage money, just for a joke." So the law had sent her some stage money, for it doesn't know anything about jokes.

I said, "Now we will call on the Principle of Forgiveness and neutralize the situation." So I said, "Infinite Spirit, we call on the Principle of Forgiveness to release this woman from the consequences of her action and give thanks that she is under divine grace and not under karmic law and cannot lose this twenty dollars, which is hers by divine right.

"Now," I said, "go back to the bank and tell them, fearlessly, that it was given to you there by mistake."

She obeyed, and to her surprise they apologized and gave her another bill, treating her most courteously.

Knowledge of this Principle gives us the power to rub out our mistakes. Some theologians and most metaphysicians say it's what made it possible for Jesus to overcome death and be resurrected. Authors Deepak Chopra and Larry Dossey, both practicing physicians, tell of cancer patients who have been freed of symptoms by applying the Principle of Forgiveness. Gerald Jampolsky, a psychiatrist, found that many of his patients were healed when they were able to experience forgiveness—both of themselves and of others.[8]

Riches

Just as we need to be free in consciousness to experience freedom in the world, if we desire riches, we must first be rich in consciousness. This is the Principle of Prosperity. And to be rich in consciousness is to live as if we already have the funds and resources we long for—not by going into debt or hoarding but by maximizing the value of what we have.

> *A woman came to me asking for treatment for prosperity. She didn't care much for housework and her home was a mess.*
>
> *I said to her, "If you wish to be rich, you must first be orderly. Everyone with great wealth is orderly and order is heaven's first law." I added, "You'll never become rich with half-full coffee cups scattered around the house."*
>
> *She had a good sense of humor and commenced putting her house in order immediately. She rearranged furniture, straightened out bureau drawers, cleaned rugs, and soon made a big financial demonstration by receiving a gift from a relative. The woman herself became made over and now keeps herself in tune financially by being ever watchful of the external and expecting prosperity, knowing that God, as divine Principle, is her supply.*

Many people are ignorant of the fact that gifts and tithes are investments and that hoarding and saving invariably lead to loss. In the Book of Proverbs, Solomon tells us, "One gives freely, yet grows all the richer; another withholds what should be given, and only suffers want."[9] He's reminding us that the richest miser lives in the poorest circumstances, and often, the gift must be given to oneself to start the flow.

> *I knew someone who wanted to buy a fur-lined overcoat. He and his wife went to various shops, but he said they were all too cheap looking. At last he was shown one that the salesman said was valued at a thousand dollars, but which the manager would sell him for five hundred dollars, as it was late in the season.*

His total financial possessions amounted to about seven hundred dollars. The reasoning mind would have said, "You can't afford to spend nearly all you have on a coat," but he was intuitive and instead turned to his wife and said, "If I get this coat, I'll make a ton of money!" So she consented, though weakly.

About a month later, he received a ten-thousand-dollar commission. The coat made him feel so rich that it linked him with success and prosperity.

Without that coat, he would not have received the commission. Investing in himself was an investment that paid large dividends!

Sadly, most people tend to ignore these intuitions to spend or to give. They miss opportunities for fulfillment by acting as if they don't have the funds. When that happens, the same amount of money will go away in an uninteresting or unhappy way, as the following example shows.

A woman told me that one Thanksgiving Day she informed her family that they could not afford a Thanksgiving dinner. She had the money but decided to save it. A few days later, someone entered her room and stole from the bureau drawer the exact amount that the dinner would have cost.

By contrast, the One Power always supports those who spend fearlessly and with wisdom by ensuring that all their needs are met.

One of my students was shopping with her little nephew and the child clamored for a toy, which she said she could not afford to buy. Then she realized suddenly that she was seeing lack and not recognizing the Infinite Source as her supply, so she bought the toy.

On her way home, she found the exact amount of money she had paid for it in the street.

This is the kind of "happy accident" that everyone is born to experience and that we can experience when we keep our eye on the Universal Principle that is working for our good, always and without fail.

Faith and Trust

In the worldly thought of the collective consciousness, there are ongoing strife and distress, but as Gautama the Buddha said, "There is an end to suffering and dissatisfaction."[10] And his teachings were designed to help us attain that end.

Worldly thought is based on ideas of sin, sickness, and death. The great spiritual teachers saw the absolute unreality of those things and told us that sickness and sorrow shall pass away and death itself may be overcome. They also taught us that our supply is inexhaustible and unfailing when we fully trust in it.

That trust, that faith, though, must precede its demonstration. In the New Testament, this is made clear: "According to your faith, be it unto you," said Jesus.[11] "Faith is the substance of things hoped for, the evidence of things not seen," said Paul.[12] Faith holds the vision steady so the adverse appearances that result from worldly thought are dissolved; it's the mind holding firm to Principle in the midst of changing circumstances. It's not a statement of belief but a deep feeling, a knowing, that what we intend will be our experience—like flipping on a light switch or opening an app on a smartphone. We have no doubt it will work just as we intend, and all our actions align with that knowing.

Undying Life

We know now from observation that death can be put off for a long time, simply by stamping the subconscious mind with the conviction of eternal youth and eternal life. At the turn of the twenty-first century, sixty is the new forty and eighty is the new sixty. Who knows what may emerge in the decades to come?

We've seen that the subconscious is power without its own direction and that it carries out the programs it's given without questioning. When the subconscious is united with and working under the direction of the superconscious, there's no logical reason why the regeneration of organs or even the resurrection of the body can't happen. Humanity could even reach a point where we no longer throw off the body in death. Instead, it would be transformed into the "body electric" sung by Walt Whitman one hundred fifty years ago.

The reclusive Kriya Yoga master Babaji is said to have been born more than five hundred years ago and to maintain the body of a teenager. His student Paramahansa Yogananda was declared dead and his body remained uncorrupted for weeks prior to its interment. Unity's founder, Charles Fillmore, lived, worked, and traveled well into his nineties, looking younger than he had at fifty and saying, "I fairly sizzle with zeal and enthusiasm," at ninety-three. These examples and more tell us that old beliefs about aging and death are just that, beliefs, and can be discarded at will.

Summary

Since the dawn of civilization, there have been tales of people who learned secrets of mind and body that allowed them to do things that other people couldn't. The early Egyptian pharaohs were expected to transform their bodies into light and leave their sarcophagi empty. The men who were called "Sons of the Sun" were expected to rise up after three days of being sealed in a tomb and then "sit at the right hand of [manage the works of] the Lord."[13] The wizards of the Middle Ages practiced alchemy to turn one material into another and their souls into pure spiritual energy. The women and men who partook of the *heiros gamos* were said to have the "gifts of the Spirit," which included being able to heal, to prophesy, and to speak so that people of many languages could understand.[14]

The people described by these stories all understood the principles we've been exploring here and trained their minds to focus only on them, raising their consciousness beyond the mental plane of the collective. We're told that on that level of consciousness, we reap where we have not sown; the gifts that are our birthright are simply poured out upon us.

Until we achieve that level, however, we experience in our lives and our world precisely what we give out in our thoughts, words, and deeds. If we judge or criticize someone, we experience ourselves being or doing precisely what we disapproved of in them; if we praise someone, we experience that. Our experience is a function of our consciousness and the consciousness of the people we relate with—the collected thoughts, feelings, beliefs, and memories that define us.

ESSENTIAL POINTS

- Our supply is inexhaustible and unfailing when fully trusted; the law always supports the person who spends fearlessly and with wisdom.
- Gifts and tithes are investments, while hoarding and saving invariably lead to loss.
- Our thoughts and actions create our circumstances.

- Freedom from all unhappy conditions comes through knowledge and application of Spiritual Principle; as with the laws of electricity, the laws of Mind obey anyone who obeys the law.

- There's a higher law than the law of Karma. Forgiveness, also known as grace, frees us from the law of cause and effect, the law of consequence, so we can reap where we have not sown and can rub out our mistakes.

- The divine pattern is the only safe pattern to work by; we should always demand only that which is ours by divine right—and that is never something that belongs to someone else.

- We always get just what we truly desire when we relinquish our personal will and enable Infinite Intelligence to work through us.

EXERCISE

Think about what saving for a rainy day means, considering the Spiritual Principle that says we cannot simultaneously claim success while preparing for failure and still expect positive results. Is there a way to turn it around and save for opportunities instead—to set aside excess funds to invest by purchasing an appreciating asset or by giving it away? What's the difference in thought and feeling between saving for emergencies and investing for opportunities?

Now consider the difference between hoarding and saving. Looking at the objects and funds you hold on to, which would you say you're doing?

Going back to the twenty-eight-day exercise you did earlier, consider the life that you would most love to be living. Are there ways you could be using the funds and other resources you currently have that would be in alignment with that life? What small actions are you ready to take, what resources are you ready to release or invest, to move your present life toward that ideal?

Write down the things you're ready to think, say, and do differently as a result of this lesson. Then, from this list and your twenty-eight-day exercise, create two or three affirmations—claims of what you intend for your life—and add them to your daily affirmations practice.

6

Casting the Burden

When we know our own power and the workings of our own mind, we discover that we really want to find a quick and easy way to impress the subconscious with programs that bring our good into our experience. By understanding that our mind is constantly reaching out into the universe to draw whatever we've been focusing on to us, we realize what we've been doing to ourselves and quickly learn that a merely intellectual knowledge of the Truth will not bring the results we seek.

In my own case, I found the easiest way is what I call *casting the burden*. It's an idea from the fifty-fifth Psalm of the Hebrew and Christian bibles, where we're told to "cast thy burden upon the Lord."

A metaphysician once explained it this way: "The only thing which gives anything weight in nature is the law of gravitation, and if a boulder could be taken high above the planet, there would be no weight in that boulder." So we need to lift our thoughts to the point where there is no more weight to them, no more gravity.[1]

From Subconscious to Superconscious

We all want to live a burden-free life, but the collective consciousness has persuaded most of us that it's impossible. The Buddha's Noble Path is designed to help us raise our consciousness out of the collective and to the centered state that comes with focusing on the superconscious mind. Jesus showed us what it's like to live that kind of life and often spoke from that risen consciousness, saying, "Come to me all you who labor and are heavy laden, and I will give you rest" and "Take my yoke upon you, for my yoke is easy and my burden is light."[2] At those times, Jesus functioned in a higher realm—a realm of vibration where there are only perfection and completion, full life and joy; where no burdens exist and where no idea of burden carries any weight.

From these teachings we can see that thoughts held in the superconscious mind are what relieve us of any burdens. Even more, we see that we violate Spiritual Principle if we hold on to a burden in our conscious or subconscious mind; it's a method of failure, just as lying is. And what is a burden? It's an adverse thought or condition in our reasoning or conscious mind that has its root in the subconscious mind.

As anyone who's tried to kick an addiction knows, it's virtually impossible to make any headway when trying to release unwanted thoughts from the conscious or reasoning mind. This is because the reasoning mind is limited and filled with the doubts and fears of the collective consciousness. It's rational, then, to cast the burden upon the superconscious mind, where all is made light and perfect and the burden is dissolved into its native nothingness.

We do this by stating with feeling, "I cast this burden of _____ on the Divine Mind within [you can use any equivalent term, such as: Christ within, Buddha Nature, inner Guru, Sacred Self, Goddess, or all-powerful superconscious mind] and I go free!"

A Christian woman in urgent need of money made the statement "I cast this burden of lack on the Christ within and I go free to have plenty!" The belief in lack was her burden, and as she cast it upon the superconscious mind, it flooded the subconscious with its belief of plenty and an avalanche of supply was the result.

In another example, one of my Unity students had been given a new piano and there was no room in her studio for it until she had moved out the old one. She was in a state of perplexity. She wanted to keep the old piano but knew of no place to keep it. She became desperate, as the new piano was to be sent immediately—in fact, was on its way. She said it came to her to repeat, "I cast this burden on the Christ within, and I go free."

A few moments later, her phone rang and a friend asked if she might rent her old piano. It was moved out just a few minutes before the new one arrived—so she not only kept the ownership of both pianos; she never had to go without one in her studio.

Yet another example addresses our inner state: I knew a woman whose burden was resentment. For years, resentment had held her in a state of torment and imprisoned her soul, her subconscious mind. She worked with me for several sessions and learned to say, with feeling, "I cast this burden of resentment on the Christ within, and I go free, to be loving, harmonious, and happy." As she did so, as she felt the release of these once cherished resentments, the Almighty superconscious flooded the subconscious with love for the people she had formerly resented and her whole life was changed.

These women experienced freedom when they released their attachment to the burden they were carrying. In twelve-step programs, this is often stated as "Let go and let God." In the Buddhist tradition, the Principle of Nonattachment is usually taught as regarding things and relationships but also applies to thought patterns.

A popular Buddhist story tells of two monks who were traveling through the countryside and came upon a stream. Standing at the edge, in the middle of the path, was a beautifully dressed young woman who asked for help getting across the water without ruining her clothes.

The older, larger monk hefted her up on his shoulders and walked across, then set her down and went on his way. The younger monk watched in amazement and then hurried to catch up with his companion.

Sometime later, seeing that the younger monk was clearly disturbed, the elder monk asked him what was on his mind. "You broke your vow and touched a woman!" the younger monk exclaimed. "How can you just keep going on?"

"Ah," the older monk said with a gentle smile, "I simply rendered a service to someone in need; no more. I put her down miles ago, but you continue to carry her!"

We all need to release the thoughts and ideas that keep us from the joy and happiness that are our birthright.

The Power of Repetition

As with most affirmations, the releasing statement should be made over and over and over, sometimes for hours at a time, silently or audibly but with determination. I've often compared it to winding up a music box or an old Victrola. We must wind ourselves up with the spoken word—repeating it until only this new set of words has meaning for us.

I've noticed, in casting the burden, that after a little while we seem to see more clearly. Our outer vision improves as the inner blinders are removed. It's impossible to have clear vision while caught up in worldly thoughts. Doubts and fear poison the mind and body, and the imagination runs riot, attracting disaster and disease in all aspects of life. As we steadily repeat the affirmation "I cast this burden on the superconscious mind and go free," the vision clears, and with it comes a feeling of relief and other experiences of good, in health, happiness, and supply.

One of my students once asked me to explain the experience that's called *the darkness before the dawn*. It's what I referred to in a preceding chapter, the fact that often, before a big demonstration of good, everything seems to go wrong and a deep depression clouds the consciousness. This kind of experience happens because the doubts and fears of past ages—in our life or the world's—are rising out of the subconscious. They have risen to the surface simply to be put out. It may sometimes seem more than we can stand, but we can and must.

And as we come to this point in the process, we're inclined to lose faith, to become distressed. But that's when we need to celebrate our freedom. We need to "clap our cymbals," like Miriam or Jehoshaphat in the Hebrew Bible stories, or beat the drum as many indigenous peoples do, and give thanks that we are saved even though we seem still surrounded by the enemy (the situation of lack, disease, or distress). Like Jesus calling Lazarus from the tomb, we give thanks that the Power is at work even before we see its results.

The student continued on, "How long must one remain in the dark?" and I replied, "Until one can see in the dark." And then I reminded her, "Casting the burden enables one to see in the dark."

Active Faith

Continually affirming is one way to establish a new belief in the subconscious, but it wouldn't be necessary to make an affirmation more than once if we had perfect faith.

To make a difference in the programs stored in the subconscious, active faith is essential. We show active faith by acting as if the thing we desire or intend is already present, as Indiana Jones does in the film *Indiana Jones and the Last Crusade* when he steps out across an abyss and the bridge appears under his feet. Elisha in the Hebrew Bible and Jesus in the New Testament showed active faith by commanding the multitude to sit down on the ground before giving thanks for the loaves and the fishes that would feed them all, despite the apparently small quantity.[3]

Through a misunderstanding, a woman had been separated from her husband, whom she loved deeply. He refused all offers of reconciliation and would not communicate with her in any way.

As she began to learn about Spiritual Principles, she denied the appearance of their separation. She made this statement: "There is no separation in Divine Mind; therefore, I cannot be separated from the love and companionship that are mine by divine right."

She showed active faith by arranging a place for them both at the table every day, thereby impressing the subconscious with a picture of his return. More than a year passed, but she never wavered, and one day he walked in.

The fact is, we're practicing active faith whenever we flip a switch to turn on a light—faith that the electrical system will work. We practice active faith whenever we place an order in a restaurant—faith that what we're hungry for will be placed before us on the table. Sadly, though, few of us are willing to practice this same faith with regard to the processes that actually make our lives work. Just as people who've never seen electricity must learn to trust that the funny little plastic thing on the wall can bring forth light elsewhere in the room, we must learn that managing our thoughts, feelings, and actions can bring forth our desired experience, both in our bodies and elsewhere in our world.

Music and Motion Can Help

The subconscious is often impressed through music. Good music played well has a quality that lifts us into a higher vibration and releases the soul from imprisonment. It makes wonderful things seem not only possible but easily accomplished!

I have a friend who plays her favorite music daily to lift her consciousness to a higher vibration. It puts her in perfect harmony with Spiritual Principles and releases her imagination to clearly see the unfolding of her intention. Another woman I know often dances while making her affirmations. The rhythm and harmony of music and motion carry her words forth with tremendous power.

When we set our affirmations to music, either through chanting or by setting them to a familiar tune, they can be very powerful indeed! In fact, much of what is considered religious music is just that: affirmations repeated with rhythm and melody. Or we can make it fun.

*For example, Myrtle Fillmore, a founder of the Unity move-
ment, used to sing, "Every little cell in my body is healthy . . .
every little cell in my body is well" to the tune of the song
"Short'nin' Bread." She was active, strong, and healthy until well
into her eighties, when one weekend she decided to pass on, went
to bed, and left her body behind; her little song is still used effectively by many today, nearly a hundred years after she created it.*

Signs of What's Coming

People who work with these principles often see small signs of
what's in process before the full demonstration of their intention
is fully manifest. We must therefore remember not to despise the
"day of small things."[4] These are welcome signs of land; before
Columbus reached America, just at the point when he was ready
to turn around, he saw birds and twigs that showed him land was
near. So it is with a demonstration; often the person doing the
work mistakes the small signs for the demonstration itself, thinking that's all that is coming and is thereby disappointed. This
disappointment then goes out and reverses the original intention,
blocking the flow of what is already theirs.

*We can see this clearly in a household example. A woman had spo-
ken the word for a set of dishes. Not long afterward, a friend gave
her a dish that was old and cracked. She came to me and said,
"Well, I asked for a set of dishes, and all I got was a cracked plate."*

*I replied, "The plate was only a sign of land. It shows your
dishes are coming—think of it as birds and seaweed," and not
long afterward, the full set of dishes arrived.*

Continually making believe is another way to impress the
subconscious. I mentioned earlier the story of a woman who

unintentionally used make-believe to ease her sorrow, but we can use it intentionally as well. Children are always making believe, and we could learn from them. "The great man is he who does not lose his child's heart," says the Chinese sage Meng Tse.[5] And Jesus told us, "Except ye become as little children, ye shall not enter the Kingdom of Heaven."[6] Both are encouraging us to rekindle our childlike openness, our childlike faith, and our childlike imaginations. If we visit beautiful places and make believe we are rich and successful, in due time we will have shifted the inner programs of the subconscious and sown enough prosperity thoughts into the universe that we will be able to reap the outer effects of our new inner state.

For instance, I know of a woman who was very poor but no one could make her feel impoverished. She earned a small amount of money from rich friends, who constantly reminded her of her poverty and told her to be careful and save.

Regardless of their admonitions, she would act as if money were not an issue in her life. She would spend all her earnings on a hat or make someone a gift and be in a rapturous state of mind the whole time. Her thoughts were always centered on beautiful clothes and rings and things that she imagined having, but without envying others.

She lived in what P. D. Ouspensky calls "the World of the Wondrous,"[7] and only riches seemed real to her. Before long she married a rich man, and the rings and things became a visible part of her daily life.

I don't know whether the man was the divine selection, but she had relied on the Principle of Opulence, so opulence had to manifest in her life.

Fear or Faith

There is no peace or happiness for any of us until we've erased all fear from our subconscious mind. Fear is misdirected energy and must be redirected, or transmuted, into Faith. The great philosopher and playwright Maurice Maeterlinck says, "Man is God afraid." And Jesus said, "Why are you fearful, O you with little faith? . . . All things are possible to those who believe."[8] Our believing does not mean we accept any one person or divinity as our God, but rather that we have a deep knowing that something is not only possible but likely—as we do when we flip a light switch or turn on our computer.

I'm asked often by my students, "How can I get rid of fear?" I reply, "By walking up to the thing you are afraid of," as did the woman with the ladder in chapter 3. Walk up to the perceived lion and it will disappear, but run away and it runs after you—the lion takes its fierceness from your fear. Remember again how the lion of lack disappeared when the person spent money fearlessly and generously.

Many of my students have come out of the bondage of poverty and are now bountifully supplied through losing all fear of letting money go out. When we give freely, the subconscious is impressed with the truth that the source of our being is both Giver and Gift. Therefore, as we are generous, the subconscious mind identifies us as one with the Giver and operates as if we are one with the Gift. A splendid statement for many is "I now thank God the Giver for God the Gift." Some prefer to say the same thing as "I am gratefully both the Source and the Receiver of infinite blessings." Both move us in the direction of that understanding.

Our thoughts of separation and lack have separated us from our good and our supply for so long that it sometimes takes spiritual dynamite to dislodge those false ideas from the subconscious.

The dynamite is often a major event. It may look like a life-threatening diagnosis or accident, a business failure, or the loss of a home—but though these may seem distressing at first, we often look back, years later, and say, "That was the best thing that ever happened to me." In our fear it looked awful; in our wisdom it looks beneficial—as is true of most events in life.

We must watch ourselves hourly to detect whether our motive for action is fear or faith. When we choose from fear, we experience more of what we're afraid of—like the man in the film *The Secret* who kept getting bills in the mail.

Perhaps you fear other people's personalities or behaviors. If so, don't avoid the people you fear; be willing to meet them cheerfully, and they will either turn out to be "golden links in the chain of one's good" or they will disappear harmoniously from your pathway.

Perhaps you fear diseases or germs. Then be fearless and undisturbed in a germ-laden situation and visualize your natural immunity. Saints in all traditions have demonstrated this principle, as have medical personnel working in leper colonies and plague-ridden communities. We can only contract the illnesses that germs carry when we vibrate at the same rate as the germ, and fear drags people down to the level of the germ. Of course, the disease-laden germ is the outer product of worldly thoughts held in the mind. Harmful germs do not exist in the superconscious or the Divine Mind; they must therefore be the product of humanity's imagination.

Freedom comes when we realize there is no power in evil. When we accept that the only power in all that exists works only for the good, the imperfections of the material world will fade away and the heavenly world, the "World of the Wondrous," will swing into view. When you become fearless, you will have completed the Game of Life!

Summary

Clearly, an essential strategy in the Game of Life is to drive out the enemies called doubt and fear from the subconscious mind. Since our subconscious mind has proven unable to eliminate fear (or anger, or pain, or resentment) from the conscious, reasoning mind, we turn instead to the superconscious, also called the Christ mind or Buddha Nature, to dissolve it. To do so requires that we operate as if we knew without a doubt that by lifting our awareness to a higher vibration, all fear-based thought and manifestation is dissolved. That's called Faith.

John's Revelation was "And I saw a new heaven, and a new earth—and there shall be no more death, neither sorrow nor crying, neither shall there be any more pain: for the former things are passed away."[9] The Buddha says that suffering and dissatisfaction must end and the wheel of Karma stop turning. It's humanity's destiny; choose Faith.

Essential Points

- When we know our own power and the workings of our mind, we realize we want to find a quick and easy way to imprint the subconscious with programs for good.
- We violate Spiritual Principle if we carry an adverse thought or condition, which is a burden, in our conscious or subconscious mind.
- It's virtually impossible to direct the subconscious to release adverse thoughts from the conscious mind, but we can cast the burden upon the superconscious mind where all is made light and burdens dissolve into their native nothingness.
- We do so by making the statement, with feeling, "I cast this burden of _____ on the superconscious mind within

and I go free!" (Or, instead of "superconscious mind," pick a term that works for you.)

- The statement of release should be made over and over and over, sometimes for hours at a time, silently or audibly but always with determination, until it has deep meaning.
- The darkness before the dawn happens when, before a big demonstration of good, everything seems to go wrong because the doubts and fears of past ages are rising out of the subconscious.
- Fear is misdirected energy and must be redirected or transformed into Faith.
- There's no peace or happiness until we've erased all fear from the subconscious mind. How can we get rid of fear? By walking up to the thing we're afraid of.

EXERCISE

Set aside a few hours one day to cast out the burden. Find a place where you can be alone and no one will be disturbed if you make noise.

Write down on a sheet of paper a fearful, angry, or resentful thought that you've been carrying about another person, yourself, or the world.

Think about all the times you've experienced people or situations related to that thought. Write down the names of all the people involved.

If you happen to remember the incident that placed that thought in your mind, describe it on the same sheet of paper—you may have been very young when it happened.

Now imagine each of those people, one by one, standing or sitting in front of you. Set the intention that this is a healing process and then tell each one everything you have to say—about them, about their role in your life, and about this thought. If strong words and feelings come up, let them. Yell at them if you need to; hit a pillow if it helps; dance or jump or stomp your feet if it gets the point across. (Don't worry about harming the people you're imagining; this is an internal process and only its results will affect the people you're focusing on.)

When you've reached the point where you have nothing more to say, tell them that you know they were doing the best they could at the time, then ask each one to forgive you for being upset at them since it happened. As you do so, feel the release. You may even imagine a beam of light shining on you and each person as you accomplish the miracle of release through the Principle of Forgiveness.

Now take the piece of paper, tear it into tiny bits, and either burn it or throw it into flowing water, saying, "It is done. I cast the burden of _____ and I am free!"

On a new sheet of paper, write the thought you intend to live from now. Write the highest, most complete truth you can think of about the situations you've been dealing with. Something like "Regardless of the form of our relationship, I know we will always be loving toward each other" or "In every situation I am poised and comfortable, and speak my most loving thoughts" or "The Universe fully supplies and supports my life and the fulfillment of my heart's desires." This is the new thought to replace the old one, so whatever you say must feel real, doable, and freeing for you, happening now and always, for the good of all.

Follow-up

Try using make-believe as another way to impress the subconscious. Take your new affirmation and imagine that your life is working that way; feel the experience as if you were actually there. Alternatively, try on the kind of clothes you'd like to be wearing, visit the beautiful buildings you intend to occupy or create more of, have tea or coffee in an expensive restaurant, write large checks for the equipment or supplies you're intending to purchase and post them where you can see them, imagine winning that race, or practice that speech or performance in front of a mirror—whatever actions will impress the subconscious that what you are affirming is, in fact, your reality.

You may also find it useful to make your new affirmation into a little song or chant. You can take a familiar tune and change it or make up your own. Or you may find that the songs and chants by various Positive Music Awards winners are useful, like Karen Drucker's "I Am So Blessed," Daniel Nahmod's "More Than Enough," Devotion's "Intention," or Karen Taylor-Good's "I Always Know What I Need to Know."[10]

7

THE PRINCIPLE OF LOVE

R eal love is selfless and free from fear. It pours itself out on the object of its affection without demanding any return. Its joy is in giving. Love is the divine made manifest, and it is the strongest magnetic force in the universe. Pure, unselfish love draws the same back to it. It does not need to seek or demand.

Every person on the planet at this time is being initiated into a higher level of love. P. D. Ouspensky states in his book *Tertium Organum* that "love is a cosmic phenomenon" that opens us to a higher-dimensional world—one he calls "the World of the Wondrous." In that world, which is our birthright, we all can know the peace of mind and joyful heart that naturally result from a life lived in love.

Scarcely anyone in the Western world has the faintest conception of real love. Living in this culture, we're too often selfish, tyrannical, or fearful in our affections, thereby losing the thing we love. And jealousy is the worst enemy of love, for the imagination runs riot, seeing the loved one as attracted to another, and invariably these fears objectify if they are not neutralized.

A woman came to me in deep distress. The man she loved had left her for another woman and said he never intended to marry her. She was torn with jealousy and resentment and said she hoped he would suffer as he had made her suffer. Then she added, "How could he leave me when I loved him so much?"

I replied, "You are not loving that man; you are hating him. You can never receive what you have never given. Give a perfect love and you will receive a perfect love. You have an opportunity to perfect yourself with this man. Give him a perfect, unselfish love, demanding nothing in return. Do not criticize or condemn him, and bless him wherever he is."

She replied, "No, I won't bless him unless I know where he is!"

"Well," I said, "that's not real love. When you send out real love, real love will return to you, either from this man or an equivalent, for if this man is not the divine selection, you will not want him. As you are human, you are one with the love that belongs to you by divine right."

Several months passed, and matters remained about the same, but she was working conscientiously with herself.

I said, "When you are no longer disturbed by his cruelty, he will cease to be cruel—you are attracting it through your own emotions."

Then I told her of people in India, who do not say, "Good morning." Instead, they use the word Namaste, *meaning "the divinity in me recognizes the divinity in you." They salute the divinity in everyone. One spiritual community uses this with even the wild animals in the jungle and the people are not harmed, for they see only God in every living thing. I said, "Salute the divinity in this man, and say, 'I see your divine self only. I see you as God sees you: perfect, made in the divine image and likeness.'"*

As she practiced the principle, she found she was becoming more poised and gradually losing her resentment. He was a captain and she always called him "the Cap." One day, she said, suddenly, "God bless the Cap, wherever he is."

I replied, "Now that is real love, and when you have become a complete circle and are no longer disturbed by the situation, you will have his love or attract its equivalent."

I was out of touch with her for a few weeks. Then one morning I received a letter saying, "We are married."

At the earliest opportunity, I called her. "What happened?" I asked.

"Oh," she exclaimed, "a miracle! One day I woke up and all suffering had stopped. I saw him that evening and he asked me to marry him. We were married in about a week, and I have never seen a more devoted husband."

The woman's husband offered her the opportunity to learn selfless love, which everyone, sooner or later, must learn.

There's an old saying: "No one is your enemy; no one is your friend; everyone is your teacher." We benefit most by becoming impersonal and learning what each person we meet has to teach us—in doing so, we can learn our lessons and be free!

Apparent Reversals

Suffering is not necessary for our development; it's the result of a violation of Spiritual Principle, but few people seem able to rouse themselves from their soul sleep without it. When people are content, they become complacent, and usually selfish, at which point the law of Karma is automatically set in action. Also, people often suffer loss through lack of appreciation, as the following example illustrates.

I knew a woman who had a very nice husband but often said, "I don't care anything about being married, but that is nothing against my husband. I'm simply not interested in married life."

She had other interests and scarcely remembered she had a husband. She only thought of him when she saw him. One day her husband told her he was in love with another woman and left. She came to me in distress and resentment.

I replied, "It's exactly what you have been affirming for years! You spoke the word for it! You said you didn't care about being married, so the subconscious worked to get you unmarried."

She said, "Oh yes, I see. People get what they've been asking for and then feel very much put out because now things are different from what they're used to, or they feel hurt because it's not what they think it should be."

The woman saw that her upset was because things had changed in a way that made her look "jilted." When she realized she was only upset because her situation didn't look the way she believed it *should* look, she realized that she wasn't really unhappy at all. She soon felt perfect harmony with the situation and knew they were both much happier apart.

When either member of a couple becomes indifferent or critical and ceases to be an inspiration to the other, it's natural that soon the other will miss the stimulation of their early relationship and become restless and unhappy. The way out is to focus on Spiritual Principle, as may be seen in the following example.

A man once came to me dejected, miserable, and poor. His wife was interested in numerology and had had his numbers read. The report was not very favorable, for he said, "My wife says I'll never amount to anything because I'm a two."

I replied, "I don't care what your number is; you are a perfect idea in Divine Mind, and we will demand the success and prosperity that are already planned for you by that Infinite Intelligence."

Within a few weeks, he had a great job, and a year or two later he achieved brilliant success as a writer.

Love and Money

Many people are kept in poverty by saying, "Money means nothing to me, and I have contempt for people who have it." This is the reason so many artists are poor. No one can attract money who despises it, and contempt for money will separate us from it. I remember hearing one artist say of another, "He's no good as an artist; he has money in the bank." This attitude separates people from their supply; we must be in harmony with a thing in order to attract it.

Money is the divine in manifestation, the divine good showing up as freedom from want and limitation, but it must always be kept in circulation and put to right uses. Hoarding and saving have their own grim vengeance. In the Gita we read, "Take care neither to acquire nor hoard. Be established in the consciousness of Atman always."

This does *not* mean that someone should not have houses and lots, stocks and bonds, for as Solomon reminded us in the Book of Proverbs, "the barns of the righteous shall be full." It does mean, however, that no one should *aim* to acquire things nor should they hoard their funds—even the principal, if an occasion arises when that money is useful for their Perfect Self-Expression. As we discovered earlier, in letting money go out fearlessly and cheerfully, we open the way for more to come in, for our supply is unfailing and inexhaustible.

This is the spiritual attitude toward money and the great Bank of Universal Supply never fails those who know and live by this Universal Principle.

The Effects of Greed

We see a powerful example of hoarding in the old silent film *Greed*. The woman won five thousand dollars (the equivalent of five million today) in a lottery but would not spend it. She hoarded and saved, let her husband suffer and starve, and eventually scrubbed floors for a living. As the film unfolds, we see that she loved the money itself and put it above everything. Then one night she was murdered and her money taken from her. Michael Douglas's role in the more recent film *Wall Street* demonstrates another way we can become monstrous when we let an attachment to money become an end in itself.

These are examples of how the love of money is the root of all evil. Money in itself can be good and beneficent but used for destructive purposes, hoarded and held on to, or considered more important than love, it brings disease, disaster, and the loss of the money itself.

All scriptural traditions say that God—as Allah, the Christ, the Lord, the I Am, the Buddha Nature, Brahman, and Atman—is essentially Love, the binding force of the Universe, and the infinite Source of all that exists is our unending supply. They show us that if we continually choose to give and receive love, all the other things we could want are added to it. But for anyone who follows the path of selfishness and greed, the supply vanishes or the person is separated from it.

I knew a very rich woman who hoarded her income. She rarely gave anything away, but bought, and bought, and bought things for herself.

She was very fond of necklaces and a friend once asked her how many she possessed. She replied, "Sixty-seven." She bought them and put them away, carefully wrapped in tissue paper, without ever wearing them.

Had she used the necklaces it would have been quite legitimate, but she was violating the Principle of Use. Her closets were filled with clothes she never wore and jewels that never saw the light.

The woman's arms gradually became paralyzed from holding on to things, and eventually she was incapable of looking after herself and her wealth was handed over to others to manage.

This is an extreme but highly illustrative example of the effects of violating Spiritual Principles with regard to wealth.

Effects of the Principle of Love

All disease and unhappiness come from the violation of the Principle of Love. The boomerangs of hate, resentment, and criticism come back laden with sickness and sorrow. So ignorance of the law brings about one's own destruction.

Love seems almost a lost art, but anyone with the knowledge of this Spiritual Principle knows it must be regained, for without it, we become empty and life becomes meaningless—as in the familiar passage on love that Paul wrote to the Christians in Corinth, we "become as sounding brass and tinkling cymbals."[1]

I had a student who came to me, month after month, to clean her consciousness of resentment. After a while she arrived at the point where she resented only one woman, but that one woman kept her busy. Little by little, however, she became poised and harmonious, and one day all of her resentment was wiped out.

That day she came in radiant and exclaimed, "You can't understand how I feel! The woman said something mean to me and instead of being furious I was loving and kind, and she apologized and was perfectly lovely to me. No one can understand the marvelous lightness I feel!"

Love and goodwill are invaluable in business as well. No one is a success in business unless they love their work. The picture painted for love of the art is the artist's greatest work. The potboiler or hack job, done just for the income, is always something to avoid. We also need to love our coworkers.

A woman came to me once, complaining about her boss. She said that her boss was cold and critical and did not want her to work there.

"Well," I replied, "salute the divinity in the woman and send her love."

She said, "I can't; she's like marble!"

I answered, "You remember the story of the sculptor who asked for a certain piece of marble. He was asked why he wanted it and replied, 'Because there is an angel in the marble,' and out of it he produced a wonderful work of art."

She said, "Very well, I'll try it." A week later she came back and said, "I did what you told me to and now the woman is very kind."

The Effects of Regret and Remorse

People are sometimes filled with remorse for having done someone an unkindness, perhaps even years ago. This is the essence of the film *Get Low*, in which a man isolates himself for forty years out of a sense of shame and guilt for a past event.

This is doubly unfortunate, as sorrow, regret, and remorse tear down the cells of the body and poison the atmosphere of the individual. But as the work of Louise Hay demonstrates, when we learn to forgive ourselves and others, our bodies and lives can be transformed.[2]

Still, the mortal mind loves to hang on to its grief and regrets. I was asked to treat a woman who was mourning for her daughter. I denied all belief in loss and separation, and affirmed that God was the woman's joy, love, and peace.

The woman gained her poise at once but sent word through her son not to treat any longer because she was "so happy, it wasn't respectable."

If the wrong can't be righted, its effect can be neutralized by doing someone a kindness in the present. This is the principle of "pay it forward," so beautifully illustrated in the book and film by that title.

Often a person's complaints are in fact a form of bragging, but this form of speaking the word carries its own results. I knew a woman who went about bragging of her troubles, so of course she always had something to brag about.

Sometimes regret or remorse takes the form of worrying about the future. The old idea was that a woman who didn't worry about her children wasn't a good mother. Now we know that mother-fear is responsible for many of the diseases and accidents that children experience. As I said previously, fear itself vividly creates pictures of the dreaded disease or situation and these pictures will become experience if they aren't neutralized. So it's important to let go of any idea that something could be wrong in our lives and in the lives of those we care about.

The Principle of Trust

Happy is the mother who can sincerely say that she puts her faith in the Divine Design and therefore knows that her children are divinely safe. In this way she throws a great aura of protection around them, an invisible protective shield. And this is so for all the people we care about.

> *A woman I know awoke suddenly in the night, feeling her brother was in great danger. Instead of giving in to her fears, she commenced making statements of Truth, saying, "Man is a perfect idea in Divine Mind and is always in the right place; therefore, my brother is in the right place and is divinely protected."*
>
> *The next day she found that her brother had been in close proximity to an explosion in a mine but had miraculously escaped.*

Clearly, we are our brother's keeper, in thought, and everyone is best served by knowing, as the Hebrew hero David did when he wrote in the Psalms that the one we love dwells in "the secret place of the most high, and abides under the shadow of the Almighty."[3] It's the Buddhist concept of sangha, the Wiccan concept of coven, the essence of community—all of us are well when we see and hold the highest good for each of our beloveds.

Summary

Love is the essential energy of the universe and all aspects of life are affected by its presence or absence. The Hebrew scriptures remind us that when we live in the vibration of love, "There shall no evil befall you, neither shall any plague come near your dwelling."[4] The New Testament assures us that "Perfect love casts out fear" and "Love is the fulfilling of the law."[5] A whole form of yoga is based on the Principle of Love, *bhakti yoga*, the path of devotion to another person or to God, and the follower of this path is assured the highest state of being, a love-bliss-consciousness called *satchidananda*, achieved through simply and fully loving. So to complete the Game of Life, we must learn to practice the art of love.

ESSENTIAL POINTS

- Every person on this planet is being initiated into a higher level of love.
- Real love is selfless and free from fear. Its joy is in giving without demanding any return.
- Love is the divine made manifest, the strongest magnetic force in the universe.
- We are often selfish, tyrannical, or fearful in our affections, thereby losing the thing we love.
- We would benefit most by not taking things personally and instead look to discover what each person we meet has to teach us—soon we would learn our lessons and be free!
- Suffering is not necessary for our development; it's the result of violation of Spiritual Principle.
- Money is the divine in manifestation as freedom from want and limitation, but it must always be kept in circulation and put to right uses. Hoarding and saving make their own grim vengeance.
- All disease and unhappiness come from the violation of the Principle of Love. The boomerangs of hate, resentment, and criticism come back laden with sickness and sorrow. These tear down the cells of the body and poison the atmosphere of the individual.

- We are all best served by knowing that the ones we love are happy, healthy, secure, and fulfilled.

Exercise

Look back over the people you've loved in your life. Starting with infancy, consider your family members and best friends; people you've dated, been engaged to, or married; had as children or helped to raise; played with on a team; had as neighbors or coworkers; met in church or temple; or saw in a movie—whomever you've felt love for, wherever and whenever.

On a sheet of paper, make a list of everyone you can remember loving, even if it was only for a few days or weeks or even if it turned sour.

Now remember how you felt when you loved them and write *I love you* next to each name. This is not a sexual or romantic statement, but a statement of Truth. And it doesn't matter what's happened between you since then—love is eternal and knows no time.

If other feelings come up as you write those words—joy, sadness, grief, pain, anger, fear, delight, peace—allow them. If you need to cast the burden, do the exercise in chapter 6.

Now put your faith in the Divine Design and imagine each of these people as divinely happy, healthy, secure, and fulfilled. Feel the peace that comes with knowing that the people you love are happy, healthy, secure, and fulfilled.

Take the sheet of paper and burn, shred, or dissolve it, releasing the past in love and claiming that the Divine Design is fulfilling the perfect pattern in your life and theirs.

8

Intuition as Guidance

There is no accomplishment too great for those who know the power of their word and follow intuitive leads. This is the essence of the great German transcendentalist philosopher Johann von Goethe's letter to his nephew:

> Concerning all acts of initiative and creation, there is one elementary truth the ignorance of which kills countless ideas and splendid plans: that the moment one definitely commits oneself and then Providence moves too. All sorts of things occur to help one that would never otherwise have occurred. A whole stream of events issues from the decision, raising in one's favor all manner of unforeseen incidents, meetings and material assistance which no man could have dreamed would have come his way.[1]

With our words we start unseen forces into action—forces that can rebuild our body or remold our circumstances. It is, therefore, of the utmost importance to choose the right words and especially important to carefully select the affirmations we wish to catapult into the invisible.

Indecision is a stumbling block in many a pathway. In order to overcome it, repeat, "I am always under direct inspiration; I make the best decisions quickly." These words impress the subconscious, and soon after performing this affirmation, a person becomes awake and alert and makes the right moves without hesitation.

Demonstrating Wealth

Through the study of Spiritual Principles, we know that our supply is infinite and constant, that there is a supply for every demand, and that our spoken word releases this supply. This is what the woman needing three thousand dollars discovered and what Jesus meant by "Ask and ye shall receive."

But we must make the first move. Once we have spoken the word, we need to pay attention to the inspirations, signs, and indications that we're being given to show us the appropriate action to take. Often these inspirations come when we're in the shower or driving long distances, because those are some of the few times we're not paying attention to someone else. Jack Canfield describes this process beautifully in the film *The Secret*, when he describes how he came to sell a large quantity of books at the beginning of his career, following the inspirations he had in the shower and meeting exactly the right person to fulfill them.

When I'm asked just how to make a demonstration, I reply, "Speak the word and then don't do anything until you get a definite lead." Demand the lead by saying, "Infinite Spirit, reveal to me the way; let me know if there is anything for me to do." We've been promised a guide for this Game, but we must call for it to appear.

The answer will come through your intuition as a hunch, a chance remark from someone, a passage in a book, a line in a movie, or any number of other places. The answers are sometimes quite startlingly precise.

> *In one case, a woman desired a large sum of money. She spoke the words "Infinite Spirit, open the way for my immediate supply; let all that is mine by divine right now reach me in great avalanches of abundance." Then she added, "Give me a definite lead. Let me know if there is anything for me to do."*
>
> *The thought came quickly: "Give _____ (a certain friend who had helped her spiritually) a hundred dollars." She told her friend, who said, "Wait and get another lead before giving it." So she waited and that very day met a woman who said to her, "I gave someone a dollar today; it was as much for me as it would be for you to give someone a hundred."*
>
> *This was indeed an unmistakable lead, so she knew she was right in giving the hundred dollars. It was a gift that proved a great investment, for shortly after that, a large sum of money came to her in a remarkable way.*

Giving opens the way for receiving. In order to create activity in finances, one should give.

Tithing, giving one-tenth of one's income, is an old Jewish custom written into the Torah to support the temple and its priesthood, the core of the community—and it's as sure a way to bring increase now as it was then. Many of the richest people in this country have been tithers, and I have never known it to fail as an investment.

The tenth goes forth and returns blessed and multiplied. But the gift or tithe must not be thought of as a duty or requirement. The goal is to feel free in the process, paying bills gratefully and sending forth all gifts and payments fearlessly and with a blessing. As the Hebrew proverb says, "God loves a cheerful giver," and the Qur'an instructs believers to give cheerfully up to a third of their income for the good of the community.

This attitude makes us the master of money. It's a form of energy that is ours to obey, and our spoken word then opens vast reservoirs of wealth.

We too often limit our supply with limited vision. By believing we're only able to manage or entitled to receive limited resources, we make it impossible for our supply to exceed that limit. We need to learn to expand our vision if we're to experience the wealth that is ours by birthright.

Then our vision and action must go hand in hand, as in the case of the man who bought the fur-lined overcoat, described in chapter 5. Sadly, though, sometimes the student of these principles has a great realization of wealth but is afraid to act.

For example, a woman came to me asking me to speak the word for a position. So I demanded, "Infinite Spirit, open the way for this woman's right position." Never ask for just "a position"; ask always for the right *position, the place already planned in Divine Mind, as it is the only one that will give you satisfaction.*

I then gave thanks that she had already received it and that it would become evident quickly. Very soon, she had three positions offered to her, two in New York and one in Palm Beach, and she did not know which to choose. I said, "Ask for a definite lead."

The time was almost up and she was still undecided when, one day, she telephoned. "When I woke up this morning, I could smell Palm Beach." She had been there before and knew its balmy fragrance.

I replied, "Well, if you can smell Palm Beach from here, it is certainly your lead." She accepted the position, and it proved a great success.

Often one's lead comes at an unexpected time like that, as once happened for me.

One day I was walking down the street when I suddenly felt a strong urge to go to a certain bakery a block or two away. The reasoning mind resisted, arguing, "There is nothing there that you want."

However, I had learned not to reason, so I went to the bakery and looked at everything, and there was certainly nothing there that I wanted, but coming out I encountered a woman I had thought of often and who was in great need of the help that I could give her at that moment.

Intuition is a spiritual faculty that does not explain but simply points the way. As a result, we often follow its guidance for one thing only to find it's for something else entirely.

People often receive a lead during a treatment. When they're listening to the practitioner speaking the word, they may be more open to receiving intuitive inspiration. When this happens, the idea that comes may seem quite irrelevant, and indeed, some of the divine leadings are mysterious. We need to override our inner censor, though, and share whatever comes up.

In class one day I was treating one of the students to receive a definite lead. A woman came to me afterward and said, "While you were treating, I got the hunch to take my furniture out of storage and get an apartment."

This woman had come to be treated for health. I told her I knew that, in getting a home of her own, her health would improve, and I added, "I believe your trouble, which is a form of congestion, may have come from having things stored away. Congestion of things causes congestion in the body. You have violated the Principle of Use, and your body is paying the penalty."

So I treated for her well-being by giving thanks that divine order was established in her mind, body, and circumstances.

Health and Circumstances as Signs

People rarely realize how their circumstances react on the body. There's a direct mental correspondence for every disease or symptom. As a result, someone might receive instantaneous healing through a realization that the body is a perfect idea in Divine Mind and, therefore, whole and perfect, but if they continue their destructive thinking, hoarding, hating, fearing, or condemning, the disease will return. The student of these principles is therefore always delving deep for the correspondence between mind and body. Louise Hay's *You Can Heal Your Life* is a wonderful resource for this process.

The aphorisms of Patanjali, a primary resource for the Hindu spiritual practice of yoga, include the statement "Pain, despair, unfortunate action, and ineffective management of life energies are the results of limitations placed in the subconscious. To overcome these obstacles and their accompaniments, focusing the will on some specific spiritual principle is required."[2]

This means a person's soul (subconscious mind) must be washed whiter than snow for permanent healing. Charles and Myrtle Fillmore, the founders of Unity, each used this principle to heal lifelong illnesses. They filled their minds with the healing ideas in the Bible and other sacred texts and wiped out any thought that they, or anyone around them, could ever act in a way that separated them from their good. As a result, she was freed of tuberculosis after years of trying various medical approaches without effect, and he restored a leg that had been shortened and deeply scarred in a childhood injury to virtually full length, strength, and function.[3] Ernest Holmes, the founder of the Centers for Spiritual Living, restored a badly cut arm in a few hours by the same principle.[4]

In the New Testament gospels, we see that this is what Jesus meant when he told people he'd healed to "go and sin no more."[5] He operated from the premise that sickness and distress came from our belief that we can sin. We understand today that this belief could be considered the ultimate limiting thought since the idea that we can sin is fundamentally the belief that we can be separated from our divine source and so be limited or lacking in our experience of the good that source is always providing.

Jesus also said, "Condemn not lest ye also be condemned," or as it is sometimes translated, "Judge not, lest ye be judged." This is an example of the principle of Karma. Many people have attracted disease and unhappiness through the condemnation of others because whatever we condemn in others, we attract to ourselves. It may be indirect, as in taking on illness, or it may be a direct reflection.

> *A friend came to me in anger and distress because her husband had deserted her for another woman. She condemned the other woman and said continually, "She knew he was a married man and had no right to accept his attentions."*
>
> *I replied, "Stop condemning the woman! Bless her and be through with the situation! Otherwise, you are attracting the same thing to yourself."*
>
> *She was deaf to my words and, a year or two later, became deeply interested in a married man herself.*

Whoever criticizes or condemns picks up a live wire—and may expect a shock.

Other Forms of Guidance

Having said that, I need to be careful with the next point. Let me say that I have found it destructive to look to the psychic plane for guidance, as it is the plane of many subjective minds, each with an opinion, and not the One Mind. The psychic plane is the result of humanity's mortal thought and is therefore a "plane of opposites." This means we may receive either good or bad messages from it.

The science of numbers and the reading of horoscopes also tend to keep people down on the mental (or mortal) plane, for these things deal only with the Karmic path—the path of probabilities that's based on the past—while the superconscious mind, operating on the plane of the One Mind, is not subject to them.

I know of someone who, according to his horoscope, should have been dead years ago but is alive and a leader of one of the biggest movements in this country for the uplifting of humanity.[6] And, in fact, there's an ancient teaching that part of our purpose in life is to overcome the limitations of the zodiac and other typologies.

It takes a strong mind to neutralize a prophecy of evil. If any such thing should occur, the student of these principles should declare, "Every false prophecy shall come to naught; every plan my superconscious mind has not planned shall be dissolved and dissipated; the divine idea, which is always my good, now comes to pass."

However, if any good message of coming happiness or wealth has ever been given, then nourish and expect it. It's in alignment with the plan of Good that is the Universal Principle and it will manifest sooner or later through the action of the subconscious mind that works to accomplish whatever we expect to experience.

Will

It's the divine will to give every one of us every righteous desire of our heart, and our will is only intended to be used to hold that perfect vision without wavering. Our will is best used to back the universal will. We can honestly say, "I will that the Universal Principle be done."

In the New Testament story known as "The Prodigal Son," a young man spends the entire inheritance he has demanded of his father and ends up working as a swineherd before he finally says, "I will arise and go to my Father." Like him, we each have to make an effort to choose to return to our true home, our true nature, the source of our birthright. It is, indeed, often an effort of the will to leave the familiar husks and swine of our past mortal thinking and return to the freedom of our true home. It seems so much easier, when starting on this path, to keep the familiar fear than turn to faith; faith is an effort of the will.

As we become spiritually awakened, though, we recognize that any external disharmony is the result of mental disharmony. If we stumble or fall in our actions, we realize that we're stumbling or falling in consciousness first.

One day, a student of these principles was walking along the street condemning someone in her thoughts. She was mentally saying, "That woman is the most disagreeable woman on earth," when suddenly three Boy Scouts rushed around the corner and almost knocked her over.

She did not condemn the Boy Scouts but saw immediately that the Principle of Karma was working and called on the Principle of

Forgiveness to free her from the karmic response to her judgment, and she then saluted the divinity in the other woman.

Wisdom's ways are ways of pleasantness and all of her paths are peace. When we've made our demands upon the Universal Principle, we must be ready for surprises. Everything may seem to be going wrong when in reality it is going right.

A woman was told that there is no loss in Divine Mind and therefore she could not lose anything that belonged to her; anything lost would be returned or she would receive its equivalent.

Several years previously, she had lost two thousand dollars. She had loaned the money to a relative, but the relative had died, leaving no mention of it in her will. The woman was resentful and angry, and as she had no written statement of the transaction, she never received the money.

Learning of Universal Principle, she determined to deny the loss and collect the money from the Bank of the Universal. She had to begin by forgiving the woman, as resentment and unforgivingness close the doors to the Universal.

She stated, "I deny loss. There is no loss in Divine Mind; therefore, I cannot lose the two thousand dollars, which belongs to me by divine right."

She was living in an apartment house that was for sale; in the lease was a clause stating that if the house were sold, the tenants would be required to move out within ninety days.

Suddenly, the landlord broke the leases and raised the rent. Again, injustice was on her path, but this time she was undisturbed. She blessed the landlord and said, "As the rent has been raised, it means that I'll be that much richer, for God is my supply."

New leases were made out for the higher rent, but by some divine mistake, the ninety-day clause had been forgotten. Soon after, the landlord had an opportunity to sell the house. On account of the mistake in the new leases, the tenants held posses- sion for another year.

The agent offered each tenant two hundred dollars if they would vacate. Several families moved and three remained, includ- ing the woman. A month or two passed and the agent again appeared. This time he said to the woman, "Will you break your lease for the sum of fifteen hundred dollars?" It flashed upon her: "Here comes the two thousand dollars." She remem- bered her friends in the house and consulted them.

These friends said, "Well, if they have offered you fifteen hundred, they will certainly give two thousand." So she remained and soon received a check for two thousand dollars for giving up the apartment. It was certainly a remarkable working of the law and the apparent injustice merely opened the way for her demonstration.

This experience proved that there is no loss, and when we use our will to maintain a spiritual stand, we collect all that is ours from this great Reservoir of Good.

We see this in the Torah, when the Lord (Universal Principle) told the tribes of Israel, "I will restore to you the years the locusts have eaten."[7] The locusts are the doubts, fears, resentments, and regrets of mortal thinking. These adverse thoughts alone rob people and the ancient principle holds true: No one gives to himself but himself, and no one takes away from himself but himself.

Summary

Humanity is here, now, to bear witness to the truth of Universal Principle so that future generations may be free of the limitations our culture has laid upon them. For as the Hebrew prophet

Malachi spoke, "Prove me now herewith, says the Lord of hosts, if I will not open for you the windows of heaven, and pour out a blessing, that there shall not be room enough to receive it." We prove that Principle by bringing plenty out of lack, health out of illness, peace out of chaos, and justice out of injustice.

We bring those conditions into our experience most readily when we claim them and allow divine inspiration, as intuition, to guide us toward the new experience. When we apply our will to keep on track with that superconscious inspiration, we avoid the obstacles and limitations of our old subconscious programs and so move effortlessly toward our perfect happiness.

ESSENTIAL POINTS

- There is no accomplishment too great for those who know the power of their own word and follow intuitive leads. Our words start unseen forces in action that can rebuild our body or remold our circumstances.

- Indecision is a stumbling block. To overcome it, repeatedly make the statement "I am always under direct inspiration; I quickly make the best decisions."

- To make a demonstration, speak the word and then don't do anything until you get a definite lead. The answer will come through your intuition as a hunch, a chance remark from someone, a passage in a book, a line in a movie or song, or any number of places.

- Giving opens the way for receiving.

- In order to create activity in finances, we need to pay out money joyfully and gratefully; our bills are to be paid cheerfully, and all money to be sent on fearlessly and with a blessing.

- Intuition is a spiritual faculty and does not explain but simply points the way—we often follow guidance thinking it's for one thing and find that it's for something else entirely.

- Whatever we condemn in others, we attract to ourselves—either directly or indirectly—so stop condemning others! Bless them and be through with the situation!
- It's the divine will to give every one of us every good and enhancing desire of our heart, and our will is only intended to be used to hold that perfect vision without wavering.

EXERCISE

Consider some circumstance in your life that you wish were different. It might be in the area of health, prosperity, relationships, work, surroundings, or spiritual experience.

Now make a list of all the people and situations you can think of who are involved with this circumstance, are doing well in a similar circumstance, or were part of previous experiences you've had like this circumstance, leaving a line between the names.

Next to each name, put an X if you have been critical or condemning in your thoughts about that person.

Now write a blessing for each person on the line below their name. It can be as simple as "I bless ..." or "God bless ..." or "Blessings of God be upon ..." or "Blessings of the Goddess ..." or "Namaste," feeling the recognition and blessing in it as you write. Or, for those you've judged against, it can be more complex: "May the life and work of _____ be blessed now and always; I release all thoughts of condemnation and I go free!" (If you find it difficult to bring yourself to write a blessing for someone, go back and do the casting the burden exercise at the end of chapter 6.)

Write a new affirmation for the circumstance, claiming the good that is your birthright, the satisfying fulfillment of your heart's desires, in accordance with the Divine Design for your life. Read it over and over until it feels true and real.

Find a way to act as if this new claim is real. If it's about prosperity, you could pay all your bills with a smiley face next to your signature and find something you can cheerfully give away. If it's about health, you could start an easy exercise routine and imagine how it feels to have the full, healthy use of your body. If it's about relationships, you could write a letter or email to yourself saying all the things you'd like to hear from someone else, or you could go out and buy a beautiful card to send to someone you care about. Feel the feelings of having the circumstance be the most wonderful experience you can imagine.

Finally, let it go. Go on with your life with as little condemnation and as many cheerful blessings as possible.

9

OUR PERFECT SELF-EXPRESSION—
THE DIVINE DESIGN

The perfect plan for fulfilling the Game of Life includes Health, Wealth, Love, and Perfect Self-Expression. This is the four-sided base of the pyramid of life, bringing perfect happiness to all who achieve it.

There's a perfect form of self-expression for each of us, something we are to do that no one else can do, a place we are to fill that no one else can fill—our destiny! It's the full expression of the unique gift I described earlier in this book.

We may not yet have the faintest idea what that action may be, for it's probably based on some marvelous talent that's hidden deep within us. But this achievement is held as a perfect idea in the Infinite Intelligence of the All, awaiting our recognition.

And because imagination is our creative faculty, we have to see the idea in our own minds before it can manifest. To experience it fully we need to say, "Infinite Spirit, open the way for the Divine Design of my life to manifest. Let the genius within me now be released. Let me see clearly the perfect plan, my perfect contribution to the All."

Keep in mind, however, that once we've made the commitment to achieve this divine perfection and actually fulfill our destiny, we may find great changes taking place in our life, for nearly everyone has wandered far from the Divine Design, manifesting jobs, relationships, and bodily conditions that are not in alignment with it. I know. In my case, it was as though a cyclone had struck my circumstances, but readjustments came quickly and new and wonderful conditions took the place of old ones.

The Easy Path

Once we've begun it, our Perfect Self-Expression will never be difficult. Instead, it will be so absorbing and interesting that it will almost seem like play—effortless, enjoyable, and energizing. When we're playing this way, nothing can stop us; we're in the zone. As the poet John Burroughs put it, "No wind can drive my bark astray nor change the tide of destiny."[1]

The student of these principles also knows that each of us comes into the world financed by the Source of all that is. All the supply needed for our Perfect Self-Expression will be at hand as we're ready for it.

Sadly, many a genius has not realized this and has struggled for years with the problem of supply when their spoken word and faith would have quickly released the necessary funds. The following story shows how this can work.

After class one day, someone came to me and handed me a penny. He said, "I have just seven cents in the world, and I'm going to give you one because I have faith in the power of your spoken word. I want you to speak the word for my perfect self-expression and prosperity."

I spoke the word and did not see him again until a year later. He came in one day, successful and happy, with a roll of bills in his pocket. He said, "Immediately after you spoke the word, I had a job offer in a distant city and am now demonstrating health, happiness, and supply."

When we demand definite signs our way will be made easy and successful. We don't need to visualize or force a mental picture to get the universe moving in support of our Perfect Self-Expression. When we demand the Divine Design to come into our conscious mind, we will receive flashes of inspiration and slowly begin to see ourselves accomplishing something great.

This is the picture or idea we must hold without wavering. It is not something that we have intentionally visualized, but rather a vision that has come to us. The thing we seek has been seeking us, just as the telephone was seeking Alexander Graham Bell and the personal computer was seeking Bill Gates, Steve Jobs, and Steve Wozniak.

Our Perfect Self-Expression could just as easily take the form of becoming the perfect partner, perfect parent, or perfect homemaker we are meant to be, or finding the perfect volunteer role to contribute to the community. It's not necessarily a public career.

This is why parents should never force careers and professions upon their children. With knowledge of spiritual Truth, the Divine Plan could be spoken for early in childhood or even prenatally. A good prenatal treatment is "Let the I Am (feel free to substitute Allah, God, Christ, Buddha Nature, Holy Spirit, Goddess, or whatever idea of the superconscious mind of all works for you) in this child have perfect expression; let the Divine Design of this little one's mind, body, and circumstances be made joyfully manifest throughout life, throughout eternity."

The Divine Plan, Not the Ego's

As we move further along in the Game, finding our Perfect Self-Expression, we long for the divine, superconscious will to be done, not the conscious ego's. "Follow the divine pattern, not the ego's pattern" is the command we find running throughout the sacred scriptures—from the Tao Te Ching to the Vedas and the sutras of Buddha and Patanjali, from the Torah to the Qur'an, and from the Zend-Avesta of the Parsees and Zoroastrians to the Bible of the Catholic, Orthodox, and Protestant Christians. They all tell us how to release our soul (or subconscious mind) from bondage, and they all teach us the science of the mind.

The battles described in so many scriptures are pictures of humanity waging war against worldly thoughts—our individual and collective effort to rid our subconscious minds of old programs that no longer serve. "Your foes shall be they of your own household" teaches the New Testament gospels. Everyone is Buddha, who turns Mara's demons' spears of suffering into flowers of peace. Everyone is David, who slays the Goliath of limited thinking with the little white stone of faith.

As Krishna tells Arjuna in the Gita, "When your intellect has cleared itself of its delusions, you will become indifferent to the results of all action, present and future."[2] With this feeling we're fearless, confident, and under direct inspiration. It means we're relying on the unlimited intelligence of the superconscious and we feel, as Jesus in the gospels did, that it is "the Father [superconscious mind] within me who does the work."[3]

I have often seen students withhold a demonstration of well-being through resistance or by insisting it can only happen one way. They pin their faith to one channel only and dictate how they desire the manifestation to come. Sadly, this behavior brings the demonstration to a standstill.

We can clearly see the difference between relying on our normal, conscious mind and relying on the superconscious in the following example.

A young boy came often to my class with his mother. He asked me to speak the word for the coming examinations at school and I told him to make the statement "I am one with Infinite Intelligence. I know everything I should know on this subject." He had an excellent knowledge of history but wasn't sure about arithmetic.

I saw him afterward and he said, "I spoke the word for my arithmetic and passed with the highest honors, but thought I could depend on myself for history and got a very poor mark."

People often receive a setback when they're too sure of themselves, which means they've been trusting their limited, conscious-mind personality and not the unlimited, superconscious individuality, the Buddha Nature or Father within.

One of my students took an extended trip abroad one summer, visiting many countries where she was ignorant of the languages. She was calling for guidance and protection every minute, and her circumstances went smoothly and miraculously. Her luggage was neither delayed nor lost. Accommodations were always ready for her at the best hotels, and she had perfect service wherever she went.

She returned to New York, and knowing the language, she felt calling for guidance was no longer necessary, so she looked after her circumstances in an ordinary manner. Everything went wrong; her luggage was delayed, and distress and confusion reigned.

The student of these principles must form the habit of what Brother Lawrence called "practicing the Presence" every minute.[4]

"In all thy ways acknowledge the divine" is a Hebrew proverb;[5] nothing is too small or too great. Sometimes a seemingly insignificant incident may be the turning point in someone's life: the inventor of the steamboat, Robert Fulton, was watching some boiling water simmering in a tea kettle when he saw the steam as a source of power.

"My way, not your way!" is the one command of Infinite Intelligence. Like all Power, it must have nonresistant instruments to work through, and we are those instruments. Like all universal principles, from electricity to gravity, it must be obeyed for us to command it.

Over and over again, we're told to stand still. In the Torah, we read this instruction to Judah and Jerusalem: "You shall not need to fight this battle; set yourselves, stand ye still, and see the salvation of the Lord with you."[6] And in the Tao Te Ching, we read, "When you do not-doing, nothing's out of order."[7]

We saw this working in the incident of the two thousand dollars coming to the woman through the landlord when she became nonresistant and undisturbed, and again when the woman won the man's love after she had cast the burden and all her suffering had ceased.

Anger, Fear, and Worry

Anger has been named one of the worst sins because its effect on us is so harmful. Anger blurs the vision, poisons the blood, is the root of many diseases, and causes decisions that lead to failure. Poised and centered in our true Self, however, we think clearly and make right decisions quickly. We never miss a clue. So the student of these principles has one goal: Poise! Poise—fearless, unwavering, focused presence—is power, for it gives divine Power a chance to rush through us, to will and do good.

The player of the Game of Life learns that the word *sin* has a much broader meaning than the traditional interpretation in our culture. The Greek word used in the New Testament to translate the Hebrew word *chata*, meaning to "go astray," was an archery term, *hamartano*, meaning "missed the mark." The English translation of that word derived from a very different Germanic root having to do with guilt. The Latin word *sin*, also present in Spanish, Italian, French, and other languages derived from Latin, means "without." Used to describe a belief in separation from our good, it becomes a far more useful and accurate way of understanding the original Hebrew concept of sin than most of us have been taught. We see that to sin is to act from the belief that we are separated from our source, our good—that we are without the good that is ours by birthright.

Fear and worry, therefore, could well be considered the real deadly sins. They are inverted faith, and through distorted mental pictures they bring the very thing we fear into our experience, too often with dreadful symptoms of distress and disease in the process.

Sadly, fear stands between us and our Perfect Self-Expression. We must be careful that we are not what Jesus called the "wicked and slothful servant" who, out of fear, buries the talent he was given.[8] There's a terrible penalty to be paid for living in fear and not using our ability.

Stage fright, for example, has hampered many a genius. When freed of it, the individual loses all self-consciousness and feels like a channel through which Infinite Intelligence expresses Itself in marvelous ways.

As we've read in the previous chapters, we can only vanquish fear by speaking the word and walking up to the thing we're afraid of. In Buddhist legends, when a bull elephant came raging through town, all others ran away but the Buddha sat quietly in its path, meditating, and the elephant stopped and knelt in front of him. In a Hebrew Bible story, when Jehoshaphat and his small army prepared to meet the enemy, singing, "Praise the Lord, for His mercy endures forever," they found that their enemies had destroyed each other, and there was no one to fight.[9] In our culture, opportunities like these are more likely to come up in the workplace or among friends.

> *A woman was asked by a friend to deliver a message to another friend. The woman feared giving the message because her reasoning mind said, "Don't get mixed up in this affair; don't give that message."*
>
> *She was troubled because she had given her word. At last, she determined to walk up to the lion and called on the Principle of Divine Protection as she did so. She met the friend to whom she was to deliver the message, and as she opened her mouth to speak it, her friend said, "So-and-so has left town." This made it unnecessary to give the message, as the situation depended upon the person being in town.*

Once again we see that as we begin to do the thing we fear, we are not obliged to; because she acted as if she did not fear, the situation vanished.

Beliefs That Delay

Some people delay demonstration of the Divine Plan in their lives through a belief in incompleteness. To overcome this, we should make the statement, "In Divine Mind there is only completion; therefore, my demonstration is completed as my perfect work, my perfect home, my perfect health, my Perfect Self-Expression."

Whatever we demand already exists as perfect ideas registered in the superconscious and must manifest under grace in a perfect way. We give thanks that we've already received on the invisible plane, and we make active preparation for receiving on the visible plane.

One of my students was in need of a financial demonstration; she came to me and asked why it was not completed. I replied, "Perhaps you're in the habit of leaving things unfinished and the subconscious has gotten into the habit of not completing—as within, so without."

She said, "You're right! I often begin things and never finish them. I'll go home and finish something I began weeks ago and I know it will be symbolic of my demonstration."

So she sewed assiduously and the project was soon completed. Shortly after, the money she was seeking came in a most curious manner: her husband was paid his salary twice that month! She said, "We told the people of their mistake, and they sent word to keep it."

When we ask, believing we are receiving, we must receive, regardless of apparent blocks in circumstances, for the Divine Plan creates its own channels.

Some people delay demonstration through indecision. I'm sometimes asked, "Suppose someone has several talents. How do we know which one to choose?" Demand to be definitely shown. Say something like "Infinite Spirit, give me a definite lead. Reveal to me my Perfect Self-Expression. Show me which talent I am to make use of now."

I have known people to suddenly enter a new line of work with little or no training and be fully equipped to do the job. Make a statement like "I am fully equipped for the Divine Plan of my life," and be fearless in grasping the opportunities that appear.

Some people are cheerful givers but bad receivers. They refuse gifts through pride or some limiting reason, thereby blocking their channels, and they invariably find themselves with little or nothing.

> *One woman who had given away a great deal of money was offered a gift of several thousand dollars. She refused to take it, saying she did not need it. Shortly after that, her finances were tied up and she found herself in debt for that amount.*

There is always a perfect balance of giving and receiving, and though we do best by giving without thinking of returns, we violate law if we do not accept the returns that come to us, for all gifts are from the Source of all that is; another person is merely the channel.

If anyone has been a bad receiver, it's time to become a good one; take even a postage stamp if it is offered, to open up the channels for receiving. Understanding the Principle of Giving and Receiving, we gratefully receive the bread returning to us upon the water, as the Hebrews do each New Year. As Jesus stated in Matthew's gospel, "Freely ye have received, freely ye shall give." He understood that when we freely exchange gifts, we build a support system of joyful interdependence. Bernard Lietaer, a former banker who now encourages a financial structure based on exchange of gifts, put it this way:

> The origin of the word *community* comes from the Latin *munus*, which means "the gift," and *cum*, which means "together, among each other." So community literally means to give among each other. Therefore, I define my

community as a group of people who welcome and honor my gifts, and from whom I can reasonably expect to receive gifts in return.[10]

In exchanging gifts, it is important to remember that a thought of lack should never be held over the giver. When my student gave me the one cent, I did not say, "Poor man—he cannot afford to give me that." I saw us both rich and prosperous, with our supply pouring in. It was this thought that brought it to him.

Two attitudes of mind cause loss: deprecation, as in the case of the woman who did not appreciate her husband, and fear of loss, which makes a picture of loss in the subconscious that then becomes the program it follows in generating our experience.

Reincarnation

I've often been asked why one person is born rich and healthy and another poor and sick. Since we can count on it that where there's an effect there is always a cause—there is no such thing as chance—this question is often answered through the Principle of Reincarnation.

As we learn to play the Game of Life, each of us goes through many births and deaths until we know the truth that sets us free. We've been drawn back to the earthly plane for many reasons: unsatisfied desire, to pay our Karmic debts, to complete a process we've set in motion, to fulfill our destiny.

Since we all manifest the sum total of our subconscious beliefs on every plane, anyone born rich and healthy can be counted on to have held pictures of health and riches in the subconscious mind prior to this life; those born poor and sick must have held images of disease and poverty.

However, birth and death themselves are human-made, for the wages of sin are death and sin is a human-made construct, explained in the Jewish, Christian, Hindu, and Muslim traditions by Adam's fall in consciousness through his made-up belief in two powers instead of One. The real person, our spirit, the Hindu and Buddhist Atman, is birthless and deathless. What Emerson called our essential Self was never born and has never died. "As was in the beginning, is now, and ever shall be!"

Summary

Through understanding the truth, we are set free from the law of Karma, sin, and death; through full self-expression, we manifest the perfect being—the divine idea, image, and likeness. Our divine path is easy, effortless, a joyful expression of the gifts we have been given. Only fear and worry can stop us. Humanity's freedom comes through each of us fulfilling our destiny, completing the Game of Life and so bringing into our experience the Divine Design of our lives.

ESSENTIAL POINTS
- The perfect plan—the fulfillment of the Game—includes Health, Wealth, Love, and Perfect Self-Expression.
- There is Perfect Self-Expression for each of us—a place we are to fill that no one else can fill, something we are to do that no one else can do: our destiny.
- Our Perfect Self-Expression will never be difficult, but of such absorbing interest that it seems almost like play—effortless, enjoyable, and energizing.
- Demand definite leads and your way will be made easy and successful. You don't need to visualize or force a mental picture; you'll receive flashes of inspiration.

- People often receive a setback when they're too sure of themselves, which means they've been trusting the limited personality and not the unlimited superconscious Mind.
- The idea of sin simply describes a belief in separation from our good, along with the actions that come from that belief.
- Fear and worry are inverted faith, and through distorted mental pictures they bring the thing we fear into our experience, along with various forms of disease and distress.
- Some people are cheerful givers but bad receivers. They refuse gifts, thereby blocking their channels, and they invariably find themselves with little or nothing. We must receive everything offered—even if it's only a postage stamp—to reopen these channels.
- As we learn to play this Game of Life, each of us goes through many births and deaths until we know the truth that sets us free.

EXERCISE

As you consider your life, if it feels somehow as though there is something yet to be done, contemplate the following until you can say it with feeling: "Infinite Spirit (or whatever term works best for you), give me a definite lead. Reveal to me my Perfect Self-Expression. Show me which talent I am to make use of now."

Say it until it feels complete, as if what you've asked for is done. Then do the same with the following: "I am fully equipped for the Divine Plan of my life." Again, say it over and over until you know that it's true. When we feel ill equipped, it's usually because we're where we do not belong, doing something that isn't ours to do.

Now, go take a shower or go out for a walk next to moving water. Plan on at least twenty minutes and up to a couple of hours. Feel the movement in your body; feel the cleansing of the old thoughts as they're replaced with a new awareness while the water flows by. Allow images and ideas to simply take form in your mind without censoring them. Let your mind go wherever it chooses rather than directing it.

When you begin to have a sense of an idea or a possibility in the direction of your fulfillment, sit down and draw or write out whatever is in your thoughts, however incomplete or unlikely. Take as long as you need to contemplate, and then draw or write what's there.

Now sit quietly, focus on something beautiful or on your breathing, and make the statement that you're ready to know what your next step is. Pay attention to the muscles in your arms and legs, notice where your focus is drawn, and note any images of people or places that appear in your mind. If your body seems to want to move, go with it. See where it takes you. If a person or place has appeared, go there and see what is there for you. Fear not, as all the angels and devas in the many sacred scriptures say, for your faith in your Perfect Self-Expression will carry you safely.

10

Wealth and Well-Being

If we are to actually experience the well-being that already exists for us, we must start with our thoughts—and the words that we speak both silently and out loud. "You, too, shall decree a thing, and it shall be established unto you" were the words that Job (*Ayyoob* in the Qur'an) heard from the Voice in the thunderstorm.[1]

As I said previously, it's very important that we think in alignment with what we intend for our lives and then word our demands correctly. We must be careful to decree in ways that ensure that only the Divine Idea is made manifest. Too often we decree our own failure or misfortune by using ill-thought words.

Decreeing

If you desire a home, friend, position, or any other good thing, make the demand for the divine selection. Try "Infinite Spirit, open the way for _____ (my right home, my right friend, my right position, and so on). I give thanks that it manifests now under grace in a perfect way." The latter part of the statement is most important, as the following story illustrates.

I knew a woman who demanded a thousand dollars. She wasn't clear about how it should come. Soon after, her daughter was injured and they received a thousand dollars from the insurance, so it did not come in a perfect way.

If she had worded the demand in this way, "Infinite Spirit, I give thanks that the one thousand dollars that is mine by divine right is now released and reaches me under grace, in a perfect way," she would not have experienced distress in the process of receiving it.

Wealth is a matter of consciousness, not activity. We must enlarge our beliefs and associated expectations in order to receive in a larger way.

The French have a legend: A poor man was walking along a road when he met a traveler who stopped and said, "My good friend, I see you are poor; take this gold nugget, sell it, and you will be rich all your days."

The man was overjoyed at his good fortune and took the nugget home. He immediately found satisfying work and became so prosperous that he did not sell the nugget.

Years passed, and he became a very rich man. One day he met a poor beggar on the road. He stopped and said, "My good friend, I will give you this gold nugget, which will make you rich for life if you sell it."

The beggar took the nugget, had it valued, and found it was only brass. So, we see, the first man became rich through feeling rich, thinking the nugget was gold.

Everyone has within himself such a gold nugget. It's our consciousness of gold, of wonderful abundance, and it brings riches into our life.

In making our demands, we begin at our journey's end; that is, we declare that we have already received.

As we grow in financial consciousness, we are ready to demand that the enormous sums of money that will enable us to transform this world and that are ours by divine right reach us under grace, in perfect ways. Sadly, though, we can't receive more than we think is possible, for we're bound by the limited programs of the subconscious. These limitations are subtle, as more than one person has discovered.

A student of these principles made the demand for six hundred dollars by a certain date. He received it but later heard that he had come very near receiving a thousand dollars. He was given just six hundred dollars as the result of his spoken word.

Praise and Thanksgiving

Ours is not to plead or supplicate but to give thanks, repeatedly, that we have received. Devout Muslims, obeying the guidelines of the Qur'an, speak praises of and thanks to Allah continuously, and especially during the five prayer periods of the day.

The Hebrew prophet Isaiah said that when we realize the living Presence of the divine, "The desert shall rejoice and blossom as the rose."[2] This rejoicing-while-yet-in-the-desert state of consciousness opens the way for release. The Protestant Christian "Lord's Prayer" is in the form of command and demand—"Give us this day our daily bread, and forgive us our debts as we forgive our debtors"—and ends in praise: "For thine is the Kingdom and the Power and the Glory forever. Amen." And as we learned earlier in this text, the Hebrew prophet Isaiah heard "Concerning the works of my hands, command ye me."[3] Prayer is command and demand, praise and thanksgiving.

Our work is to make ourselves believe that with God (Allah, Atman, the Goddess, the infinite Source of all that is—whatever term helps you feel the power and presence) all things are possible. This is easy enough to state in the abstract but a little more difficult when confronted with a problem.

It was necessary for a woman to demonstrate a large sum of money within a stated time. She knew she must do something to get a realization (realization is "to make real" in our experience) and demanded a lead.

She was walking through a department store when she saw a very beautiful, pink-enamel letter opener. She felt the pull toward it. The thought came: "I don't have a letter opener good enough to open letters containing large checks."

So she bought the letter opener, which the reasoning mind would have called an extravagance. When she held it in her hand, she had a flash of herself opening an envelope containing a large check, and in a few weeks she received the money. The pink letter opener was her ditch in the desert, her bridge of active faith.

Many stories are told of the power of the subconscious when directed in faith.

A very powerful one involves a man who was spending the night in a farmhouse. The windows of the room had been nailed down, and in the middle of the night he felt suffocated and made his way in the dark to a window. He could not open it so he smashed the pane with his fist, drew in draughts of fine, fresh air, and had a wonderful night's sleep.

The next morning, he found he had smashed the glass of a bookcase and the window had remained closed the whole night.

He had supplied himself with oxygen simply by his thought of oxygen.

One of my students once made the wonderful statement "When I ask the Father for anything, I put my foot down and I say, 'Father, I'll take nothing less than what I've asked for, but I'll gladly take more!'"

Likewise, we should never compromise. We follow Paul's guidelines to the Christians in Ephesians and "Having done all, stand."

This is sometimes the most difficult stage in the process. The temptation comes to give up, to turn back, to compromise. But once we start, we must never turn back. Our demonstrations often come at the eleventh hour because that's when we finally let go—that is, stop our conscious reasoning and give Infinite Intelligence a chance to work. An old saying goes, "Man's dreary desires are answered drearily, and our impatient desires long delayed or violently fulfilled."

This may apply to great things or small, as was the case when one woman asked me why she was constantly losing or breaking her glasses. In the course of our conversation, we found she often said to herself and others, with vexation, "I wish I could get rid of my glasses." So her impatient desire was violently fulfilled.

What she really wanted was perfect eyesight, but what she registered in the subconscious was simply the impatient desire to be rid of her glasses, so they were continually being broken or lost. A more effective statement would have been "The perfect thought in Divine Mind makes my eyesight so good that I no longer need glasses."

When a student of these principles is able to let go of a problem with feeling (casting a burden), instantaneous manifestation is the result. For example, a woman was out during a very stormy day and her umbrella was blown inside out. She was about to call on some people whom she had never met and she did not wish to make her first appearance with a dilapidated umbrella. She could not throw it away, as it did not belong to her. So in desperation, she exclaimed, "God, you take charge of this umbrella. I don't know what to do!"

A moment later, a voice behind her said, "Lady, do you want your umbrella mended?" There stood an umbrella mender.

She replied, "Indeed, I do."

The person mended the umbrella while she went into the house to pay her call, and when she returned she had a good umbrella.

So there is always an umbrella mender at hand, on our pathway, when we put the umbrella (or our situation) in the Divine Hands.

Denials Followed by Affirmations

Many thoughts that have not served us, and appearances that don't feel in alignment with our good, may be erased by simply denying their truth. One should always follow a denial—claiming the appearance as nothingness—with an affirmation, the claim of a more perfect design.

I was called on the phone late one night to treat someone whom I had never seen. He was apparently very ill. As usual, I first entered the silence, unifying the conscious and superconscious mind, and then I made the statement "I deny this appearance of

disease. It is unreal, therefore cannot register in our consciousness;
this man is a perfect idea in Divine Mind, pure substance
expressing perfection."

The next morning I was told that he was much better, and
the following day out attending to business.

There is no time or space in Infinite Intelligence. Therefore
the word instantly reaches its destination and does not return
void. I have treated patients in Europe while sitting in New York
and have found that the results were instantaneous.

Visualizing and Visioning

I am asked so often the difference between visualizing and visioning, and the answer is this: visualizing is a mental process
governed by the reasoning or conscious mind; visioning is a spiritual process governed by intuition, or the superconscious mind.

We need to train the conscious mind to receive these flashes
of inspiration and work out the divine pictures that have been
received through definite leads, signs, or clues as to our best
next step.

Spiritual traditions encourage us to give up worldly desires.
They're not saying that we should give up appreciating the gifts
and experiences that come with living. Their goal is for us to
stop limiting ourselves to the pleasures and possibilities we've
been programmed to live for and instead allow ourselves the
unlimited bliss that is the Divine Plan for us.

Many of us are building a bungalow for ourselves, in imagination, when we could be building a palace, because we limit
ourselves through reason. When we can truly say, "I desire only
that which is in the Divine Plan for me," our false desires, based
on shoulds and reasons, fade from consciousness and a new set of

blueprints is given to us by the Master Architect, also known as the superconscious or God within. The Divine Plan for each person transcends the limitation of the reasoning mind and is always the four-sided square of the complete life: Health, Wealth, Love, and Perfect Self-Expression.

More than that, if you try to force a demonstration through the reasoning mind, it comes to a standstill. To fulfill the Divine Plan, we should act only through intuition or definite leads. The old Hebrew guideline still applies: "Rest in the Lord [Spiritual Principle] and wait patiently. Trust also in him, and He will bring it to pass."

I have seen the Principle work in the most astonishing manner. One of my students stated that it was necessary for her to have a hundred dollars by the following day. It was a debt of vital importance that had to be met. I spoke the word, declaring Spirit was never too late and that the supply was at hand.

That evening she phoned to tell me of a miracle. She said that the thought came to her to go to her safety-deposit box at the bank to examine some papers. She looked over the papers, and at the bottom of the box was a new one-hundred-dollar bill.

She was astounded and said she knew she had never put it there, since she'd gone through the papers many times.

It may have been a form of demonstration we call *materialization*—something that didn't exist before our treatment now does, as Elijah materialized oil for the widow in the Hebrew Bible and Jesus materialized the loaves and fishes in the New Testament. We will reach the stage where our own word is also instantly materialized, as happens with the great saints and avatars of all spiritual traditions.

Naming the Divine

There is a tremendous power in simply saying the Divine Name. For Muslims, for example, simply saying "Allah" is the most powerful statement that can be made.

For Hindus and Buddhists, the all-encompassing consciousness is *Om*. The very sound of the word lifts our vibration, and in a *sangha*, "where two or more are gathered,"[4] chanting it from the resonant depths of their being, all are lifted even higher.

For Christians the name of power is Jesus Christ, which is a combination of the Hebrew name *Yeshua*, also written *Joshua*, meaning "Savior, Deliverer," and a Greek word created by early Christians to describe the idea of Messiah, derived from *chrestos*, which means "best, highest." The name stands for Truth Made Manifest. The gospels tell us, "Whatsoever ye ask the Father, in my name, He will give it to you."[5] Its power raises the student of these principles to a higher vibration, where we are freed from all astral and psychic influences, and we become "unconditioned and absolute."[6] I have seen many healings accomplished simply by using the words, "In the name of Jesus Christ."

The Christ was both person and principle, and the Christ Principle within each of us is our Redeemer (redeeming, accepting, and transforming that which we release) and Salvation (bringing fulfillment, completion, and wholeness). Christ is a term describing our own higher-vibration Self, our superconscious being, functioning in the divine image and likeness. This is the Self that Ralph Waldo Emerson told us to rely on in his essay "Self-Reliance." It's the Self that has never failed, never known sickness or sorrow, was never born, and has never died. It works outside of space and time to alter conditions and bring to us that which is ours by decree and divine right.

The Hindus call this deathless aspect of being Atman. And just as Jesus is the embodiment of the Christ, Krishna is the embodiment of Atman. Some have said they are the same person, returning from age to age and culture to culture so that humanity may know the truth and be freed.

By whatever name we know it, by whatever images and prayers and practices we use to experience it, the Source of All That Is constantly unfolds, through and as all beings, always. How could it be otherwise?

Summary

All power is given to each of us, through effective thinking and speech, to bring our own heaven upon our world. This is the ultimate goal of the Game of Life. We do it by reprogramming the subconscious so that its operating system, which coordinates the acting out of our individual behavior patterns and programs, is based on eternal Spiritual Principles rather than our limiting beliefs.

The clues and indicators are in our bodies, our lives, and our world —as above, so below; as without, so within. The simple rules may be found in the one place most people will never look: our own inner wisdom. They've been discovered by a few in each culture and shared in the sacred writings called scriptures, and are based on nonresistance, fearless faith, and loving goodwill.

The Game is already underway, and you *will* win. Only the time it takes you to do so may vary.

So, may you now be freed from whatever has held you in bondage through the ages, standing between you and your own, and may you know the Truth that makes all beings free. I speak the word and it is so. You, dear reader, are free to fulfill your destiny, to win the Game, bringing into your experience the Divine

Design of your life: Health, Wealth, Love, and Perfect Self-Expression. And I give thanks that this is so, now and always.

ESSENTIAL POINTS

- Wealth is a matter of consciousness. We must enlarge our beliefs and associated expectations in order to receive in a larger way.

- If you desire a home, friend, position, or any other good thing, make the demand for the divine selection to ensure that the result most fully meets your highest good.

- Continually affirming is one way to establish a new belief in the subconscious. It wouldn't be necessary to make an affirmation more than once if we had the perfect faith we have in a light switch!

- Ours is not to plead or supplicate, but to give thanks, repeatedly, that we have received. Prayer is command and demand, praise and thanksgiving.

- Once a student of these principles starts out to demonstrate, s/he should never turn back. Demonstrations often come at the eleventh hour because that's when we finally let go—that is, stop our conscious reasoning and give Infinite Intelligence a chance to work.

- Visualizing is a mental process governed by the reasoning or conscious mind; visioning is a spiritual process governed by intuition, or the superconscious mind.

- We should always follow a denial—claiming the appearance as nothingness—with an affirmation—the claim of a more perfect design.

- All the spiritual traditions encourage us to stop limiting ourselves to the pleasures and possibilities we've been programmed to live for and instead allow ourselves the unlimited bliss that is the Divine Plan for us.

- There is a tremendous power in simply saying the Divine Name. The power of this name, in whatever tradition we follow, raises the student of these principles to a higher vibration, where we are freed from all astral and psychic influences, and we become "unconditioned and absolute."
- All power is given to each of us through effective thinking and speech to bring our own heaven upon our world. This is the goal of the Game of Life.

EXERCISE

Set aside an hour or so in a place where you'll be comfortable, and make sure you have some paper and something to write with nearby.

Sit quietly for a minute or two with your eyes closed and simply pay attention to your breathing.

Remember your bedroom. Visualize the doorway and the bed, the drawers and shelves, the window with its covering, the light fixture. See the colors and the textures of the various objects and notice what's on the floor. Remember how the floor feels under your feet and how the bedcovering feels to your hand.

Now breathe and refocus your inner vision.

Remember someplace you've visited that you would really enjoy visiting again. Visualize the entry and the space. See the colors and textures and feel them with your hands and feet. Remember what it felt like to enter the space and imagine that you're doing so now.

When you've experienced a clear image of the space, take a deep breath and get up and move your body around a bit; then settle in comfortably, closing your eyes again. (You may find that taking a bath or shower, or walking by flowing water, or even driving in the country works better for you than sitting in a comfortable place—that's fine. Whatever works!)

This time, ask the question: What is the highest and best thing that I could be doing next? Then, sit quietly for a minute or two and pay attention to your breathing.

A thought or image may come to mind; allow it. Breathe into it. Fill your inner vision with it. Then return to your breathing.

If the image persists as you return to your breathing, follow it. Where does it lead you? If it leads you to the past or your to-do list, or if it's uncomfortable, open your eyes and write it down and return to your breathing.

Ask again, "What is the highest and best thing that I could be doing next?" Then, sit quietly for a minute or two and pay attention to your breathing. This time, smile as you breathe.

Again, allow whatever thought or image comes to your mind. Breathe into it. Fill your inner vision with it. Then return to your breathing. If the image persists as you return to your breathing, follow it. When you've gone as far as you comfortably can with it, open your eyes and write it down.

The apparently random thoughts and images forming in your mind as you ask this question are indicators of the direction in which you're ready to move—and that direction will be effortless, enjoyable, and energizing.

If it isn't clear what your next step is in manifesting this vision, you're ready for a lead, something that you see or hear that points you in the most effective direction. Command the Infinite Intelligence that resides within your being to show you the next step in a way you can easily recognize it.

Now go about whatever you normally do, confident that the highest and best way for you to move forward in the Game of Life is being made clear to you.

Some Effective Affirmations

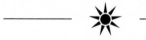

For Prosperity

The Source of all is my unfailing supply, and large sums of money and abundant resources come to me quickly, under grace, in perfect ways.

Infinite Spirit opens the way for _____. I give thanks that it manifests now, under grace, in a perfect way.

For Right Conditions

Every plan that's not in the Divine Design shall be dissolved and dissipated, and the Divine idea for the well-being of all now comes to pass.

Only that which is true of the Source of All is true of me, for the Source and I are one.

Divine Love now dissolves and dissipates every wrong condition in my mind, body, and circumstances. Divine Love is the most powerful chemical in the universe, dissolving everything that is not of itself!

For Faith

As I am one with my Source, and the Source of all is good, I am one with my good.

For Guidance

I am divinely sensitive to my intuitive leads, and I give instant obedience to the Divine Will—which is for my perfect well-being.

I see clearly the open way; there are no obstacles on my pathway.

I see clearly the perfect plan.

I am always receiving Divine Inspiration; I make decisions quickly and for the best possible outcome for all.

For Health

Divine Love floods my consciousness with health, and every cell in my body is filled with light.

Infinite Intelligence brings all the cells, organs, and tissues of my body into perfect harmony and function so that all processes work smoothly for my perfect well-being.

For Eyesight

My eyes are the Divine eyes; I see with the eyes of Spirit.

The perfect thought in Divine Mind makes my eyesight so good that I no longer need glasses.

For Hearing

My ears are the Divine ears; I hear with the ears of Spirit. I am nonresistant, and I am willing to be led. I hear glad tidings of great joy.

The perfect thought in Divine Mind makes my hearing so good that I no longer need hearing aids.

For Right Work

I do _____ in a _____ way; I give _____ service for _____
pay. (Use "perfect" or some other word that works for you to fill
in the blanks: ideal, delightful, wonderful, and so on.)

For Freedom from All Bondage

I cast this burden on the Infinite Intelligence and Power within,
and I go free!

A Summary of the Principles

Principle of Cause and Effect—for every effect there is a cause; material events are never the cause

Principle of Consequence—for every thought, word, or action there is a consequence

Principle of Divine Protection—because there is in reality no evil and nothing harmful, we are fully protected in all circumstances

Principle of Forgiveness—we all have the power to forgive or neutralize our mistakes and those of others

Principle of Giving and Receiving—they are the same; we receive what we give, must give to receive, and must receive to open the flow

Principle of Love—love is the binding force of the universe and our lives, and no other power exists

Principle of Nonresistance—like water, which transforms objects by flowing around them, we accomplish the greatest things by not doing anything about a circumstance except to think the highest blessing that we can for it

Principle of Opulence—in order to demonstrate our truly abundant supply, we must first feel that we have received abundantly

Principle of Prosperity—our supply is always present, and we can reveal, through our spoken word, all that belongs to us as our inalienable birthright

Principle of Reflection—what we perceive is a function of our mental framework, so to quote the ancients, "As without, so within"; and in the modern twelve-step movement, "If you spot it, you've got it"

Principle of Reincarnation—each of us goes through many births and deaths learning to play this Game of Life, until we know the truth which sets us free

Principle of Substitution—when a right idea is substituted for a wrong one, there is no loss or sacrifice

Principle of Transmutation, founded on nonresistance—through our spoken word alone, every failure is transmuted into success

Principle of Use—use it or lose it

Science Relating to
The Game of Life

Over the past several decades, more and more experimental researchers have been exploring concepts related to the ideas introduced in *The Game of Life*. Two of the best-known, most rigorous laboratories doing this work are the Institute of Noetic Sciences and the Institute of HeartMath, both now located in Northern California. In addition, the National Science Foundation and the National Institutes of Health have been funding a number of projects in universities and independent laboratories that tend to support these ideas. What follows is an overview of some of these experiments as they relate specifically to Shinn's work.

The Power of Love

Perhaps the most important and fundamental point in Shinn's work is that our lives are happier, healthier, and more prosperous when we let go of past fears and resentments and replace them with loving thoughts and feelings—toward ourselves and toward the people around us.

The physical effects of love and appreciation have been well established in the laboratory for some time. Researchers at the Institute of HeartMath have demonstrated that ongoing positive emotions, such as appreciation, love, or compassion, are associated with highly ordered or coherent patterns in heart rhythms. In general, they observed that heart-focused attention is correlated with greater synchronization of heart and brain. This *physiological coherence* leads to a state of "more ordered and harmonious interactions among the body's systems." They also found that when individuals were taught how to use a positive-emotion refocusing technique to generate appreciation (such as affirmations), coherence among organs and systems in the body significantly increased.[1]

The effects of affectionate bonding between people are also well established. For example, successful sports-team members refer to a "sixth sense" empathy and an ability to "anticipate the moves of the other" or to a "click of communality," an almost audible shift whereby sports participants "react as a . . . unit, rather than as an aggregate of individuals."[2]

And it turns out that these bonds have effects on the four-legged creatures we call our friends. In a series of studies done around the world using synchronized timers and video recorders, pets at home changed their activity when their owners began to return home from work or an excursion, even when the time of return varied from day to day.[3]

Intention also plays a significant role in the effects experienced. In the case of sports teams, the intention is to work together effectively to accomplish a goal. In other studies, the intention is that one or more people experience greater health— we call this prayer, or sometimes "spiritual healing." One comparison of *131 controlled studies involving prayer or spiritual healing found that 77 (59 percent) showed statistically significant results.*[4]

The Power of Forgiveness and Casting the Burden

Shinn tells us that we can overcome many current problems by releasing past resentments and current beliefs. She calls this "casting the burden." Her ideas were based on both biblical references and the experiences she and her students had; for her they were clear demonstrations that we can release and be done with certain patterns of thought and feeling and move on into new life experiences—ones that are no longer affected by those thoughts and feelings.

For at least two thousand years, the process of forgiving oneself and others has been offered as a way to empowerment and a sense of well-being. It's the essence of the Christian message and was deeply woven into the Greek mystery-school tradition, as carried on through the Freemasons. In recent years, therapists have rediscovered its effectiveness—largely due to the emergence of the twelve-step movement, with its emphasis on atoning and making amends, as well as the work Victor Frankl and others have done with victims of the Nazi Holocaust. Psychologists, psychiatrists, and counselors have since applied it to address both individual and collective trauma.[5]

Additional research suggests that there is a link between relief of symptoms from some chronic and acute conditions and letting go the burden of emotional memories or the sense of responsibility.[6]

In general, using a variety of tests, researchers have found that "positive spiritual experiences and willingness to forgive are related to better physical health." They've also found that "negative spiritual experiences are related to worse physical and mental health for individuals with chronic disabilities," reinforcing the idea that forgiving, or releasing negative past experiences, is conducive to health and well-being.[7]

The Power of the Spoken Word, Thoughts, Feelings, and Beliefs

Shinn's work was based almost entirely on her demonstrated experience that clear statements of belief and intention, free of conflicting beliefs, change an individual's body and circumstances. She knew this logically, from an understanding of Spiritual Principles, and experientially, in her own life and in the lives of her students. Recently, scientists from a number of disciplines have discovered the physiological processes that occur in the body when we speak or feel intensely.

Back in the 1970s, a researcher at the National Institutes of Health rocked the world with her discovery of "molecules of emotion." Candace Pert's research on neuropeptides established that certain chemicals manufactured in the brain were present throughout the body and affected the operation of various cells when triggered by a signal from the brain.[8] This process is illustrated beautifully in the film *What the Bleep Do We Know!?* and its sequel, *What the Bleep!?: Down the Rabbit Hole.*

With that study, Pert established what Shinn had been teaching: that our bodies react immediately and powerfully to what we think, feel, and say—and that the unconscious function has no capacity to distinguish between what's imagined and what's experienced.

Biochemist Bruce Lipton explored the mechanism of that process in his research on the structure and activity of the cell membrane, as described in his book *The Biology of Belief* and numerous articles. He became convinced that cell processes were determined by the activity of millions of receptors on the cell membrane, and that while most of that activity was chemical, a good deal of it was the result of energy fields. Specifically, through a process known as *electro-conformational coupling*, resonant vibrational energy fields can alter the balance of charges in a protein, causing the cell to accept that protein molecule as a different molecule![9] He also demonstrates that in a harmonic energy field, cell receptors will change their conformation and so accept different molecules than they used to. This means that cell activity is affected by both chemicals like the neuropeptides that Candace Pert discovered and by energy fields like the ones that Rollin McCraty and others at the Institute of HeartMath discovered.

Shinn understood this, in principle, almost a hundred years ago when she encouraged people not to be as concerned about germs and medications as about the thoughts and feelings they were holding.

While the cell membrane determines the activities of a cell, the DNA stored in the nucleus determines the way the cell reproduces—and may do much more. Russian researchers exploring the 90 percent of DNA on the human chromosome that Western researchers describe as "junk" found that these unexplored molecules act like information processors in a computer. In their experiments, they demonstrated that DNA substance in living tissue (but not in test tubes or petri dishes) reacts to laser beams and radio waves that are modulated with language. Using this method, the Russian group repaired chromosomes that had been damaged by X-rays, among other things.

The fact that our DNA reacts to language explains why affirmations, autogenous training, hypnosis, and the like can have such strong effects on humans and their bodies. The trick is that the frequency pattern of the beam carrying the words has to be correct for the words to work, which explains why not everybody is equally successful or can always achieve the same results. The individual must develop inner processes to establish a frequency of thought that permits communication with the

DNA.[10] As spiritual teachers through the ages as well as Florence Shinn have encouraged, we need to practice not only "speaking the word," but also feeling it, from a mental state in which we feel connected to the source of our being.

The Russian research also helps explain why the Institute of HeartMath's experimental evidence suggests that certain prolonged negative psychological states encourage the progression of cancer and increase risk for physical illness and early death.[11] It also validates Shinn's statement that negative thoughts and feelings, over time, work their way into physical expression in the body.

Researchers using Random Number Generators (RNG) in computers—programs that produce a 1 or a 0 with no pattern or equation to them—have demonstrated conclusively that not only do individuals affect equipment like heart monitors and electroencephalograms (EEG), but we can intentionally or unconsciously affect the operation of all kinds of electronic equipment. And we can do so as individuals and as a group. Computer operators have played with RNGs since the beginning of computing, seeing if they could affect the sequence, create a pattern, even create a picture on a screen or printout full of 1s and 0s. The Global Consciousness Project at Princeton University was established to see what effect major events that involved many people might have on a set of RNGs spread out and connected by the internet. They had shown a number of statistically significant results through the years 1994 through early 2001, but went off the map, literally, on September 11, 2001. At that time, as project director Dean Radin puts it, "all randomness went away shortly before the event and was restored a few days after."[12] So what we're feeling not only affects our bodies but also the electronic equipment around us, and it works in synergy with the feelings of others to affect equipment located nowhere near us.

As we consider this in light of what Shinn has been telling us, we realize that our thoughts and feelings really do have an impact on the world around us. It's most evident in machines that are basically moving electrons around, but all things are made up of moving electrons, so we must affect everything!

The Process of Intuition

Shinn tells us that our most effective action is that which is based on inspiration and intuition. Intuitive awareness and the following of "signs" and "leads" are skills she encourages us to develop. She's quite clear that our reasoning mind often leads us astray, while a quiet mind, centered on Spiritual Principles, is open to receiving information from what she calls Infinite Intelligence—information that will help us in all our endeavors and ensure our health, happiness, and prosperity.

There have been hundreds of books and thousands of articles written about ways to improve one's intuition. Most of these are based on the positive experiences of the author and the author's students in applying their methods. That fact alone suggests that it is worth exploring.

Rigorous application of the scientific method to the concept of intuition, however, has some limiting issues. First of all, what is the definition of intuition? Second, what process exactly are we testing for? Third, how do we separate memory and sensory input from intuitive input?

Physicists Russell Targ and Hal Puthoff decided to address some of these issues in the 1970s by placing their subjects in a Faraday cage, a space that's been shielded from all sorts of electromagnetic input. They then gave their subjects a piece of paper with a set of letters or numbers on it and asked them to describe or sketch what they saw in their mind's eye. The results were consistently and powerfully astounding: people with little or no known training, and with nothing more than a few letters or numbers, were consistently able to describe or sketch the essentials—and sometimes substantial details—of the locations or the objects in those locations that the letters or numbers related to.[13] This process, traditionally called *clairvoyance*, later became known as *remote viewing* and became part of the US intelligence-gathering process into the 1990s.

Charles Tart, one of the first modern researchers to apply rigorous scientific methods to the field of consciousness research, developed the concept of "discrete states of consciousness." He found in his explorations of these states that when two subjects hypnotized each other, they claimed to know each other's thoughts and feelings.[14]

Ken Wilber, a writer and philosopher who integrates other people's theories and findings, has identified three possible ways these kinds of results can be achieved:

1. A direct communication between people, usually called telepathy or psychic communication

2. A transcendent field or mind that incorporates all human minds (called by Ralph Waldo Emerson the Over-Soul, by Ernest Holmes the Divine Mind, by most Christians the Holy Spirit, and described by Lynn McTaggart in her book *The Field*)[15]

3. A harmonic resonance between individuals such that what is happening in one mind is also happening in another mind with similar energy patterns (also called Morphic Resonance by Rupert Sheldrake in his book *A New Science of Life*)[16]

There is no clear scientific explanation for how any of these may work, but theoretical physicist Amit Goswami has proposed that the underlying fabric of the universe is itself conscious and that since we emerge out of and are part of that fabric, our consciousness is interwoven with it—and with each other.[17] This means that all beings can tap into what Shinn called Infinite Intelligence at any time—because we are it.

NOTES

INTRODUCTION

1. For an introduction to Hopkins's teachings, see Ruth L. Miller's *Unveiling Your Hidden Power: Emma Curtis Hopkins' Metaphysics for the 21st Century* (Portland, OR: WiseWoman Press, 2005).

2. This is why the pyramid on the Great Seal of the United States is unfinished—we've not yet completed ourselves.

CHAPTER 1

1. You may have heard this legend before. There are different versions in different countries but they all say that the divine beings that created humanity knew that human beings could become just like them if we knew the Truth, so they decided to hide it. Different versions have different stories about their various attempts, but they all end up with it being hidden in our hearts—the last place we'd ever look for our own capacity to, as the New Testament says, "be as gods."

2. Qur'an, Surah 1:1–7.

3. Ursula K. Le Guin, "Verse #10," *Lao Tzu: The Tao Te Ching: A Book about the Way and the Power of the Way* (Boston: Shambhala, 1998).

4. Wayne Dyer, *Your Sacred Self: Making the Decision to Be Free* (New York: Harper-Collins, 1996).

5. Available in several sources: Coleman Barks, *The Essential Rumi* (New York: HarperSanFrancisco, 2004); also online on various websites with Rumi quotes.

6. New Testament, 1 Timothy 4:14.

7. Bhagavad Gita, chapter 2.

8. Bhagavad Gita, chapter 9.

9. Hebrew Bible, Isaiah 45:11.

10. New Testament, Matthew 7:7.

11. Modern brain research has demonstrated that it takes a minimum of twenty-eight days for a neural connection to shift from one set of neurons in the brain to another. See Science Relating to *The Game of Life* at the end of the interpretation for more information.

CHAPTER 2

1. Wendell Phillips (1811–84), "The Lesson of the Hour: Harper's Ferry" speech, delivered in Brooklyn, NY, November 1, 1859; transcribed in *Speeches, Lectures, and Letters, Series One* (1863), Google Books online, 279.

2. Hebrew Bible, Numbers 13:33.

3. Hebrew Bible, 1 Corinthians.

4. New Testament, Acts 5; John 11:1–45.

5. New Testament, Matthew 18:20.

CHAPTER 3

1. New Testament, Matthew 12:37.

2. This is the opening line of most translations of the Qur'an. It has a parallel in Judaism: "Hear O Israel, the Lord your god is One."

3. William H. Murray, *The Scottish Himalayan Expedition* (1951).

4. Louise Hay, *Heal Your Body A–Z: The Mental Causes for Physical Illness and the Way to Overcome Them* (New York: Hay House, 1984); Hay, *You Can Heal Your Life* (Hay House, 1984). Both have sold millions of copies and show the relationship between specific symptoms and their related emotional states.

5. New Testament, John 13: 34–35.

6. New Testament, Matthew 10:36.

7. Hebrew Bible, Deuteronomy 6:5; New Testament, Luke 10:27, Matthew 12:29.

8. New Testament, Matthew 5:11.

9. Hebrew Bible, Isaiah 54:17.

CHAPTER 4

1. New Testament, Matthew 16:23.

2. Emma Curtis Hopkins, "Lesson Two," *Scientific Christian Mental Practice* (Camarillo, CA: DeVorss & Company, 1974); Miller, *Unveiling Your Hidden Power: Emma Curtis Hopkins' Metaphysics for the 21st Century* (Portland, OR: WiseWoman Press, 2005).

3. Ralph Waldo Emerson, the essay "Spiritual Laws" in various texts, including *Natural Abundance: Ralph Waldo Emerson's Guide to Prosperity*, edited by Ruth L. Miller (Hillsboro, OR: Beyond Words, 2011).

4. *Satyagraha* is a Sanskrit term loosely translated as "insistence on truth satya (truth) agraha (insistence) soul force." Mohandas Gandhi invented the term to describe the particular way he had found to work best in resisting the British. As he wrote in his 1928 booklet *Satyagraha in South Africa*, "Truth (satya) implies love, and firmness (agraha) engenders and therefore serves as a synonym for force. I thus began to call the Indian movement Satyagraha, that is to say, the Force which is born of Truth and Love or nonviolence, and gave up the use of the phrase 'passive resistance' in connection with it." The famous Salt March illustrated in the Richard Attenborough film *Gandhi* is a beautiful example of the concept.

5. New Testament, Matthew 5:25.

6. Qur'an 41:34.

7. New Testament, 2 Corinthians 6:2.

CHAPTER 5

1. Bhagavad Gita, chapter 3.

2. Bhagavad Gita, chapter 5.

3. New Testament, Luke 23:43.

4. Psalms 111:10; Proverbs 9:10.

5. New Testament, John 8:32.

6. Bhagavad Gita, chapter 2.

7. Hebrew Bible, Exodus 14:13.

8. Gerald G. Jampolsky and Neale Donald Walsch, *Forgiveness: The Greatest Healer of All* (Hillsboro, OR: Atria/Beyond Words, 1999); Gerald. G Jampolsky, *Teach Only Love: The Twelve Principles of Attitudinal Healing* (Atria/Beyond Words, 2000).

9. Proverbs 11:24.

10. This is the second Noble Truth generally ascribed to Gautama Buddha when he began his teachings.

11. New Testament, Matthew 9:29.

12. New Testament, Hebrews 1:16.

13. New Testament, Mark 16:19, carried forward from Psalm 110 in the Hebrew Bible. Aramaic scholar George Lamsa, in *Light on the Gospels*, explains that this is an idiom meaning "manages the work of."

14. New Testament, I Corinthians, chapters 12 and 28 describe "gifts of the spirit"; "fruits of the spirit" are described in Galatians, 5:22.

Chapter 6

1. This is not to say there would be no mass in that boulder but that it would be weightless. Having the mass of a boulder, it would take some energy to move it, but without weight it would not be a burden.
2. New Testament, Matthew 11:28–36.
3. The story of the loaves and fishes is in all four gospels in one form or another.
4. Hebrew Bible, Zechariah 4:10.
5. The Mencius, Book IV.
6. New Testament, Matthew 18:3.
7. P. D. Ouspensky, *Tertium Organum* (New York: Alfred Knopf, 1922).
8. New Testament, Mark 9:23.
9. New Testament, Revelation 21.
10. These and hundreds of others of songs may be found online at www.empower ma.com.

Chapter 7

1. New Testament, I Corinthians 13.
2. Louise Hay, *Heal Your Body A–Z: The Mental Causes for Physical Illness and the Way to Overcome Them* (New York: Hay House, 1984); Hay, *You Can Heal Your Life* (Hay House, 1984).
3. Hebrew Bible, Psalm 91:1.
4. Hebrew Bible, Psalm 91:10.
5. New Testament, 1 John 4:18.

Chapter 8

1. William H. Murray, *The Scottish Himalayan Expedition* (1951).
2. Verses 36 and 37 in the first book of *The Yoga Sutras of Patanjali*, originally written between 1600 and 600 BCE. This is a transliteration of many translations, including ones by Christopher Isherwood, Alice Bailey, and Archibald Bahm.
3. James Dillet Freeman, *The Story of Unity* (Summit, MO: Unity Press, 1993); Charles Braden, *Spirits in Rebellion* (Dallas, TX: Southern Methodist University Press, 1984).
4. Ruth L. Miller, *A Power Beyond Magic: The Extraordinary Life of Ernest Holmes* (Portland, OR: WiseWoman Press, 2007).
5. New Testament, all four gospels.
6. She's referring to Charles Fillmore, who cofounded Unity in 1893 and lived and actively worked well into his nineties using these principles and practices.
7. Hebrew Bible, Joel 2:25.

Chapter 9

1. John Burroughs, "My Own Shall Come to Me," publication unknown.
2. Bhagavad Gita, chapter 2.
3. New Testament, John 14:10.
4. Brother Lawrence, *The Practice of the Presence of God the Best Rule of a Holy Life* (Gloucester, UK: Dodo Press, 2007).
5. Hebrew Bible, Proverbs 3:6.
6. Hebrew Bible, 2 Chronicles 20:17.
7. Ursula K. Le Guin, "Verse #3," *Lao Tzu: The Tao Te Ching: A Book About the Way and the Power of the Way* (Boston: Shambhala, 1998).
8. New Testament, Matthew 25:26.
9. Hebrew Bible, 2 Chronicles 20.
10. Interview with Bernard Lietaer, author of *The Future of Money: Creating New Wealth, Work, and a Wiser World* (London: Random House, 2001), www.lietaer.com.

Chapter 10

1. Hebrew Bible, Job 22:28.
2. Hebrew Bible, Isaiah 35:1.
3. Hebrew Bible, Isaiah 45:11.
4. New Testament, Matthew 18:20.
5. New Testament, John 16:23.
6. Immanuel Kant, *Critique of Pure Reason* (Cambridge, UK: Cambridge University Press, 1999). In this text, Kant describes the fundamental qualities of anything that might be called God.

Science Relating to The Game of Life

1. Rollin McCraty, *The Energetic Heart: Bioelectromagnetic Interactions Within and Between People* (Boulder Creek, CA: Institute of HeartMath, 2003).
2. Michael Murphy and R. A. White, *The Psychic Side of Sports* (Boston: Addison-Wesley, 1978).
3. Rupert Sheldrake, *Dogs That Know When Their Owners Are Coming Home and Other Unexplained Powers of Animals* (New York: Three Rivers Press, 1999).
4. Daniel Benor, "Survey of Spiritual Healing Research." *Complementary Medical Research* 4:1, 1990.
5. A substantial list of research papers for the years 2007–2009 may be found on www.forgivenessresearch.com.
6. Lynn B. Myers, "Treatments for Cystic Fibrosis: The Role of Adherence, Importance and Burden." *Cystic Fibrosis: Etiology, Diagnosis and Treatments* (Hauppauge,

NY: Nova Press, 2009), 185–97; E. L. Worthington Jr. and G. Sotoohi, "Physiological Assessment of Forgiveness, Grudges, and Revenge: Theories, Research Methods, and Implications." *International Journal of Psychology Research*, 5.3–4 (2011): 291–316.

7. B. Johnstone and D. P. Yoon, "Relationships between the Brief Multidimensional Measure of Religiousness/Spirituality and Health Outcomes for a Heterogeneous Rehabilitation Population." *Rehabilitation Psychology*, 54 (2009): 422–31.

8. Candace Pert, *Molecules of Emotion: The Science Behind Mind-Body Medicine* (New York: Simon & Schuster, 1999).

9. T. Tsong, "Trends in Biochemical Studies." *Science*, 14 (1989): 89–92.

10. Grazyna Gosar and Franz Bludorf, *Vernetzte Intelligenz* [Networked Intelligence] (Aachen, Germany: Omega-Verlag Gisela Bongart und Martin Meier GbR, 2001).

11. Rollin McCraty, *The Energetic Heart: Bioelectromagnetic Interactions Within and Between People* (Boulder Creek, CA: Institute of HeartMath, 2003).

12. Dean Radin, "Exploring Relationships Between Random Physical Events and Mass Human Attention Asking for Whom the Bell Tolls." *Journal of Scientific Exploration*, 16:4 (2002), 533–47.

13. Russell Targ and Harold Puthoff, *Mind-Reach: Scientists Look at Psychic Abilities* (New York: Dell Publishing, 1977).

14. Charles Tart, "Psychedelic Experiences Associated with a Novel Hypnotic Procedure, Mutual Hypnosis." C. Tart (ed.), *Altered States of Consciousness* (New York: John Wiley, 1969, 291–308).

15. Lynn McTaggart, *The Field: The Quest for the Secret Force of the Universe* (New York: HarperCollins, 2002).

16. Ken Wilber, *A Theory of Everything: An Integral Vision for Business, Politics, Science, and Spirituality* (Boston: Shambhala, 2007).

17. Amit Goswami, *The Self-Aware Universe* (New York: Tarcher, 1995); Goswami, *The Physicists' View of Nature: The Quantum Revolution* (New York: Kluwer Associates/Plenum Publishing, 2001).

ORIGINAL TEXT

————

As Published in 1925

1

THE GAME

Most people consider life a battle, but it is not a battle, it is a game.

It is a game, however, which cannot be played successfully without the knowledge of spiritual law, and the Old and the New Testaments give the rules of the game with wonderful clearness. Jesus Christ taught that it was a great game of *Giving and Receiving*.

"Whatsoever a man soweth that shall he also reap." This means that whatever man sends out in word or deed, will return to him; what he gives, he will receive.

If he gives hate, he will receive hate; if he gives love, he will receive love; if he gives criticism, he will receive criticism; if he lies he will be lied to; if he cheats he will be cheated. We are taught also, that the imaging faculty plays a leading part in the game of life.

"Keep thy heart (or imagination) with all diligence, for out of it are the issues of life." (Prov. 4:23.)

This means that what man images, sooner or later externalizes in his affairs. I know of a man who feared a certain disease. It was a very rare disease and difficult to get, but he pictured it continually and read about it until it manifested in his body, and he died, the victim of distorted imagination.

So we see, to play successfully the game of life, we must train the imaging faculty. A person with an imaging faculty trained to image only good, brings into his life "every righteous desire of his heart"—health, wealth, love, friends, perfect self-expression, his highest ideals.

The imagination has been called, "*The Scissors of The Mind*," and it is ever cutting, cutting, day by day, the pictures man sees there, and sooner or later he meets his own creations in his outer world. To train the imagination successfully, man must understand the workings of his mind. The Greeks said: "Know Thyself."

There are three departments of the mind, the *subconscious, conscious* and *superconscious*. The subconscious, is simply power, without direction. It is like steam or electricity, and it does what it is directed to do; it has no power of induction.

Whatever man feels deeply or images clearly, is impressed upon the subconscious mind, and carried out in minutest detail.

For example: a woman I know, when a child, always "made believe" she was a widow. She "dressed up" in black clothes and wore a long black veil, and people thought she was very clever and amusing. She grew up and married a man with whom she was deeply in love. In a short time he died and she wore black and a sweeping veil for many years. The picture of herself as a widow was impressed upon the subconscious mind, and in due time worked itself out, regardless of the havoc created.

The conscious mind has been called mortal or carnal mind.

It is the human mind and sees life as it *appears to be*. It sees death, disaster, sickness, poverty and limitation of every kind, and it impresses the subconscious.

The *superconscious* mind is the God Mind within each man, and is the realm of perfect ideas.

In it, is the *"perfect pattern"* spoken of by Plato, *The Divine Design*; for there is a *Divine Design* for each person.

"There is a place that you are to fill and no one else can fill, something you are to do, which no one else can do."

There is a perfect picture of this in the *super-conscious mind*. It usually flashes across the conscious as an unattainable ideal—"something too good to be true."

In reality it is man's true destiny (or destination) flashed to him from the Infinite Intelligence which is *within himself*.

Many people, however, are in ignorance of their true destinies and are striving for things and situations which do not belong to them, and would only bring failure and dissatisfaction if attained.

For example: A woman came to me and asked me to "speak the word" that she would marry a certain man with whom she was very much in love. (She called him A. B.)

I replied that this would be a violation of spiritual law, but that I would speak the word for the right man, the "divine selection," the man who belonged to her by divine right.

I added, "If A. B. is the right man you can't lose him, and if he isn't, you will receive his equivalent." She saw A. B. frequently but no headway was made in their friendship. One evening she called, and said, "Do you know, for the last week, A. B. hasn't seemed so wonderful to me." I replied, "Maybe he is not the divine selection—another man may be the right one." Soon after that, she met another man who fell in love with her at once, and who said she was his ideal. In fact, he said all the things that she had always wished A. B. would say to her.

She remarked, "It was quite uncanny."

She soon returned his love, and lost all interest in A. B.

This shows the law of substitution. A right idea was substituted for a wrong one, therefore there was no loss or sacrifice involved.

Jesus Christ said, "Seek ye first the Kingdom of God and his righteousness; and all these things shall be added unto you," and he said the Kingdom *was within man.*

The Kingdom is the realm of *right ideas,* or the divine pattern.

Jesus Christ taught that man's words played a leading part in the game of life. "By your words ye are justified and by your words ye are condemned."

Many people have brought disaster into their lives through idle words.

For example: A woman once asked me why her life was now one of poverty of limitation. Formerly she had a home, was surrounded by beautiful things and had plenty of money. We found she had often tired of the management of her home, and had said repeatedly, "I'm sick and tired of things—I wish I lived in a trunk," and she added: "Today I am living in that trunk." She had spoken herself into a trunk. The subconscious mind has no sense of humor and people often joke themselves into unhappy experiences.

For example: A woman who had a great deal of money, joked continually about "getting ready for the poorhouse."

In a few years she was almost destitute, having impressed the subconscious mind with a picture of lack and limitation.

Fortunately the law works both ways, and a situation of lack may be changed to one of plenty.

For example: A woman came to me one hot summer's day for a "treatment" for prosperity. She was worn out, dejected and discouraged. She said she possessed just eight dollars in the world. I said, "Good, we'll bless the eight dollars and multiply them as Jesus Christ multiplied the loaves and the fishes," for He taught that every man had the power to bless and to multiply, to heal and to prosper.

She said, "What shall I do next?"

I replied, "Follow intuition. Have you a 'hunch' to do anything, or to go anywhere?" Intuition means, intuition, or to be taught from within. It is man's unerring guide, and I will deal more fully with its laws in a following chapter.

The woman replied: "I don't know—I seem to have a 'hunch' to go home; I've just enough money for carfare." Her home was in a distant city and was one of lack and limitation, and the reasoning mind (or intellect) would have said: "Stay in New York and get work and make some money." I replied, "Then go home— never violate a hunch." I spoke the following words for her: "*Infinite Spirit open the way for great abundance for* _____. *She is an irresistible magnet for all that belongs to her by divine right.*" I told her to repeat it continually also. She left for home immediately. In calling on a woman one day, she linked up with an old friend of her family.

Through this friend, she received thousands of dollars in a most miraculous way. She has said to me often, "Tell people about the woman who came to you with eight dollars and a hunch."

There is always *plenty on man's pathway*; but it can only be *brought into manifestation* through desire, faith or the spoken word. Jesus Christ brought out clearly that man must make the *first move*.

"*Ask*, and it shall be given you, seek, and ye shall find, knock, and it shall be opened unto you." (Mat. 7:7.)

In the Scriptures we read:

"Concerning the works of my hands, command ye me."

Infinite Intelligence, God, is ever ready to carry out man's smallest or greatest demands.

Every desire, uttered or unexpressed, is a demand. We are often startled by having a wish suddenly fulfilled.

For example: One Easter, having seen many beautiful rose-trees in the florists' windows, I wished I would receive one, and for an instant saw it mentally being carried in the door.

Easter came, and with it a beautiful rose-tree. I thanked my friend the following day, and told her it was just what I had wanted.

She replied, "I didn't send you a rose-tree, I sent you lilies!"

The man had mixed the order, and sent me a rose-tree simply because I had started the law in action, and *I had to have a rose-tree.*

Nothing stands between man and his highest ideals and every desire of his heart, but doubt and fear. When man can "wish without worrying," every desire will be instantly fulfilled.

I will explain more fully in a following chapter the scientific reason for this and how fear must be erased from the consciousness. It is man's only enemy—fear of lack, fear of failure, fear of sickness, fear of loss and a feeling of *insecurity on some plane.* Jesus Christ said: "Why are ye fearful, oh ye of little faith?" (Mat. 8:26.) So we can see we must substitute faith for fear, for fear is only inverted faith; it is faith in evil instead of good.

The object of the game of life is to see clearly one's good and to obliterate all mental pictures of evil. This must be done by impressing the subconscious mind with a realization of good. A very brilliant man, who has attained great success, told me he had suddenly erased all fear from his consciousness by reading a sign which hung in a room. He saw printed, in large letters this statement—"*Why worry, it will probably never happen.*" These words were stamped indelibly upon his subconscious mind, and he has now a firm conviction that only good can come into his life, therefore only *good can manifest.*

In the following chapter I will deal with the different methods of impressing the subconscious mind. It is man's faithful servant but one must be careful to give it the right orders. Man has ever a silent listener at his side—his subconscious mind.

Every thought, every word is impressed upon it and carried out in amazing detail. It is like a singer making a record on the sensitive disc of the phonographic plate. Every note and tone of the singer's voice is registered. If he coughs or hesitates, it is registered also. So let us break all the old bad records in the subconscious mind, the records of our lives which we do not wish to keep, and make new and beautiful ones.

Speak these words aloud, with power and conviction: "I now smash and demolish (by my spoken word) every untrue record in my subconscious mind. They shall return to the dust-heap of their native nothingness, for they came from my own vain imaginings. I now make my perfect records through the Christ within—the records of *Health, Wealth, Love and perfect self-Expression.*" This is the square of life, *The Game completed.*

In the following chapters, I will show how man can change his conditions by changing his words. Any man who does not know the power of the word is behind the times.

"*Death and Life are in the power of the tongue.*" (Prov. 18:21.)

2

THE LAW OF PROSPERITY

*Yea, the Almighty shall be thy defense and thou shalt
have plenty of silver.*

One of the greatest messages given to the race through the
scriptures is that God is man's supply and that man can
release, *through his spoken word*, all that belongs to him by divine
right. He must, however, have *perfect faith in his spoken word*.

Isaiah said, "My word shall not return unto me void, but shall
accomplish that where unto it is sent." We know now, that words
and thoughts are a tremendous vibratory force, ever molding
man's body and affairs.

A woman came to me in great distress and said she was to be
sued on the fifteenth of the month for three thousand dollars.
She knew no way of getting the money and was in despair.

I told her God was her supply, and *that there is a supply for
every demand.*

So I spoke the word! I gave thanks that the woman would
receive three thousand dollars at the right time in the right way.
I told her she must have perfect faith, and act her *perfect faith.* The
fifteenth came but no money had materialized.

She called me on the 'phone and asked what she was to do.

I replied, "It is Saturday, so they won't sue you today. Your part is to act rich, thereby showing perfect faith that you will receive it by Monday." She asked me to lunch with her to keep up her courage. When I joined her at a restaurant, I said, "This is no time to economize. Order an expensive luncheon, act as if you have already received the three thousand dollars."

"All things whatsoever ye ask in prayer, *believing*, ye shall receive." "You must act as if you had *already received*." The next morning she called me on the 'phone and asked me to stay with her during the day. I said "No, you are divinely protected and God is never too late."

In the evening she 'phoned again, greatly excited and said, "My dear, a miracle has happened! I was sitting in my room this morning, when the doorbell rang. I said to the maid: 'Don't let anyone in.' The maid, however, looked out the window and said, 'It's your cousin with the long white beard.'

"So I said, 'Call him back. I would like to see him.' He was just turning the corner, when he heard the maid's voice, and *he came back.*

"He talked for about an hour, and just as he was leaving he said, 'Oh, by the way, how are finances?'

"I told him I needed the money, and he said, 'Why, my dear, I will give you three thousand dollars the first of the month.'

"I didn't like to tell him I was going to be sued. What shall I do? I won't *receive it till* the first of the month, and I must have it tomorrow." I said, "I'll keep on 'treating.'"

I said, "Spirit is never too late. I give thanks she has received the money on the invisible plane and that it manifests on time." The next morning her cousin called her up and said, "Come to my office this morning and I will give you the money." That afternoon, she had three thousand dollars to her credit in the bank, and wrote checks as rapidly as her excitement would permit.

If one asks for success and prepares for failure, he will get the situation he has prepared for. For example: A man came to me asking me to speak the word that a certain debt would be wiped out.

I found he spent his time planning what he would say to the man when he did not pay his bill, thereby neutralizing my words. He should have seen himself paying the debt.

We have a wonderful illustration of this in the bible, relating to the three kings who were in the desert, without water for their men and horses. They consulted the prophet Elisha, who gave them this astonishing message:

"Thus saith the Lord—Ye shall not see wind, neither shall ye see rain, yet make this valley full of ditches."

Man must prepare for the thing he has asked for, *when there isn't the slightest sign of it in sight.*

For example: A woman found it necessary to look for an apartment during the year when there was a great shortage of apartments in New York. It was considered almost an impossibility, and her friends were sorry for her and said, "Isn't it too bad, you'll have to store your furniture and live in a hotel." She replied, "*You needn't feel sorry for me, I'm a superman, and I'll get an apartment.*"

She spoke the words: "*Infinite Spirit, open the way for the right apartment.*" She knew there was a supply for every demand, and that she was "unconditioned," working on the spiritual plane, and that "one with God is a majority."

She had contemplated buying new blankets, when "the tempter," the adverse thought or reasoning mind, suggested, "Don't buy the blankets, perhaps, after all, you won't get an apartment and you will have no use for them." She promptly replied (to herself): "I'll dig my ditches by buying the blankets!" So she prepared for the apartment—acted as though she already had it.

She found one in a miraculous way, and it was given to her although there were over *two hundred other applicants.*

The blankets showed active faith.

It is needless to say that the ditches dug by the three kings in the desert were filled to over-flowing. (Read, II Kings.)

Getting into the spiritual swing of things is no easy matter for the average person. The adverse thoughts of doubt and fear surge from the subconscious. They are the "army of the aliens" which must be put to flight. This explains why it is so often, "darkest before the dawn."

A big demonstration is usually preceded by tormenting thoughts.

Having made a statement of high spiritual truth one challenges the old beliefs in the subconscious, and "error is exposed" to be put out.

This is the time when one must make his affirmations of truth repeatedly, and rejoice and give thanks that he has already received. "Before ye call I shall answer." This means that "every good and perfect gift" is already man's awaiting his recognition.

Man can only receive what he sees himself receiving.

The children of Israel were told that they could have all the land they could see. This is true of every man. He has only the land within his own mental vision. Every great work, every big accomplishment, has been brought into manifestation through holding to the vision, and often just before the big achievement, comes apparent failure and discouragement.

The children of Israel when they reached the "Promised Land," were afraid to go in, for they said it was filled with giants who made them feel like grasshoppers. "And there we saw the giants and we were in our own sight as grass-hoppers." This is almost every man's experience.

However, the one who knows spiritual law, is undisturbed by appearance, and rejoices while he is "yet in captivity." That is, he holds to his vision and gives thanks that the end is accomplished, he has received.

Jesus Christ gave a wonderful example of this. He said to his disciples: "Say not ye, there are yet four months and then cometh the harvest? Behold, I say unto you, lift up your eyes and look on the fields; for they are ripe already to harvest." His clear vision pierced the "world of matter" and he saw clearly the fourth dimensional world, things as they really are, perfect and complete in Divine Mind. So man must ever hold the vision of his journey's end and demand the manifestation of that which he has already received. It may be his perfect health, love, supply, self-expression, home or friends.

They are all finished and perfect ideas registered in Divine Mind (man's own superconscious mind) and must come through him, not to him. For example: A man came to me asking for treatments for success. It was imperative that he raise, within a certain time, fifty-thousand dollars for his business. The time limit was almost up, when he came to me in despair. No one wanted to invest in his enterprise, and the bank had flatly refused a loan. I replied: "I suppose you lost your temper while at the bank, therefore your power. You can control any situation if you first control yourself." "Go back to the bank," I added, "and I will treat." My treatment was: "You are identified in love with the spirit of everyone connected with the bank. Let the divine idea come out of this situation." He replied, "Woman, you are talking about an impossibility. Tomorrow is Saturday; the bank closes at twelve, and my train won't get me there until ten, and the time limit is up tomorrow, and anyway they won't do it. It's too late." I replied, "God doesn't need any time and is never too late. With Him all things are possible." I added, "I don't know anything about business, but I know all about God." He replied: "It all sounds fine when I sit here listening to you, but when I go out it's terrible." He lived in a distant city, and I did not hear from him for a week, then came a letter. It read: "You were right.

I raised the money, and will never again doubt the truth of all that you told me."

I saw him a few weeks later, and I said, "What happened? You evidently had plenty of time, after all." He replied "My train was late, and I got there just fifteen minutes to twelve. I walked into the bank quietly and said, 'I have come for the loan,' and they gave it to me without a question."

It was the last fifteen minutes of the time allotted to him, and Infinite Spirit was not too late. In this instance the man could never have demonstrated alone. He needed someone to help him hold to the vision. This is what one man can do for another.

Jesus Christ knew the truth of this when he said: "If two of you shall agree on earth as touching anything that they shall ask, it shall be done for them of my Father which is in heaven." One gets too close to his own affairs and becomes doubtful and fearful.

The friend or "healer" sees clearly the success, health, or prosperity, and never wavers, because he is not close to the situation.

It is much easier to "demonstrate" for someone else than for one's self, so a person should not hesitate to ask for help, if he feels himself wavering.

A keen observer of life once said, "no man can fail, if some one person sees him successful." Such is the power of the vision, and many a great man has owed his success to a wife, or sister, or a friend who "believed in him" and held without wavering to the perfect pattern!

3

THE POWER OF THE WORD

By thy words thou shalt be justified,
and by thy words thou shalt be condemned.

A person knowing the power of the word becomes very careful of his conversation. He has only to watch the reaction of his words to know that they do "not return void." Through his spoken word, man is continually making laws for himself.

I knew a man who said, "I always miss a car. It invariably pulls out just as I arrive."

His daughter said: "I always catch a car. It's sure to come just as I get there." This occurred for years. Each had made a separate law for himself, one of failure, one of success. This is the psychology of superstitions.

The horseshoe or rabbit's foot contains no power, but man's spoken word and belief that it will bring him good luck creates expectancy in the subconscious mind, and attracts a "lucky situation." I find, however, this will not "work" when man has advanced spiritually and knows a higher law. One cannot turn back, and must put away "graven images." For example: Two men in my class had had great success in business for several months, when suddenly everything "went to smash." We tried to analyze the situation, and I found, instead of making their affirmations and looking to God for success and prosperity, they had each bought a "lucky monkey." I said: "Oh, I see, you have been trusting in the lucky monkeys instead of God. Put away the lucky monkeys and call on the law of forgiveness," for man has power to forgive or neutralize his mistakes.

They decided to throw the lucky monkeys down a coalhole, and all went well again. This does not mean, however, that one should throw away every "lucky" ornament or horseshoe about the house, but he must recognize that the power back of it is the one and only power, God, and that the object simply gives him a feeling of expectancy.

I was with a friend, one day, who was in deep despair. In crossing the street, she picked up a horseshoe. Immediately, she was filled with joy and hope. She said God had sent her the horseshoe in order to keep up her courage.

It was indeed, at that moment, about the only thing that could have registered in her consciousness. Her hope became faith, and she ultimately made a wonderful demonstration. I wish to make the point clear that the men previously mentioned were depending on the monkeys, alone, while this woman recognized the power back of the horseshoe.

I know, in my own case, it took a long while to get out of a belief that a certain thing brought disappointment. If the thing happened, disappointment invariably followed. I found the only way I could make a change in the subconscious, was by asserting, "There are not two powers, there is only one power, God, therefore, there are no disappointments, and this thing means a happy surprise." I noticed a change at once, and happy surprises commenced coming my way.

I have a friend who said nothing could induce her to walk under a ladder. I said, "If you are afraid, you are giving in to a belief in two powers, Good and Evil, instead of one. As God is absolute, there can be no opposing power, unless man makes the false of evil for himself. To show you believe in only One Power, God, and that there is no power or reality in evil, walk under the next ladder you see." Soon after, she went to her bank. She wished to open her box in the safety-deposit vault, and there stood a ladder on her pathway. It was impossible to reach the box without passing under the ladder. She quailed with fear and turned back. She could not face the lion on her pathway. However, when she reached the street, my words rang in her ears and she decided to return and walk under it. It was a big moment in her life, for ladders had held her in bondage for years. She retraced her steps to the vault, and the ladder was no longer there! This so often happens! If one is willing to do a thing he is afraid to do, he does not have to.

It is the law of nonresistance, which is so little understood.

Someone has said that courage contains genius and magic. Face a situation fearlessly, and there is no situation to face; it falls away of its own weight.

The explanation is that fear attracted the ladder on the woman's pathway, and fearlessness removed it.

Thus the invisible forces are ever working for man who is always "pulling the strings" himself, though he does not know it. Owing to the vibratory power of words, whatever man voices, he begins to attract. People who continually speak of disease invariably attract it.

After man knows the truth, he cannot be too careful of his words. For example: I have a friend who often says on the 'phone, "Do come to see me and have a fine old-fashioned chat." This "old-fashioned chat" means an hour of about five hundred to a thousand destructive words, the principal topics being loss, lack, failure and sickness.

I reply: "No, I thank you, I've had enough old-fashioned chats in my life, they are too expensive, but I will be glad to have a new-fashioned chat, and talk about what we want, not what we don't want." There is an old saying that man only dares use his words for three purposes, to "heal, bless or prosper." What man says of others will be said of him, and what he wishes for another, he is wishing for himself.

"Curses, like chickens, come home to roost."

If a man wishes someone "bad luck," he is sure to attract bad luck himself. If he wishes to aid someone to success, he is wishing and aiding himself to success.

The body may be renewed and transformed through the spoken word and clear vision, and disease be completely wiped out of the consciousness. The metaphysician knows that all disease has a mental correspondence, and in order to heal the body one must first "heal the soul."

The soul is the subconscious mind, and it must be "saved" from wrong thinking.

In the twenty-third psalm, we read: "He restoreth my soul." This means that the subconscious mind or soul, must be restored with the right ideas, and the "mystical marriage" is the marriage of the soul and the spirit, or the subconscious and super-conscious mind. They must be one. When the subconscious is flooded with the perfect ideas of the superconscious, God and man are one. "I and the Father are one." That is, he is one with the realm of perfect ideas; he is the man made in God's likeness and image (imagination) and is given power and dominion over all created things, his mind, body and affairs.

It is safe to say that all sickness and unhappiness come from the violation of the law of love. A new commandment I give unto you, "Love one another," and in the Game of Life, love or good-will takes every trick.

For example: A woman I know, had, for years an appearance of a terrible skin disease. The doctors told her it was incurable, and she was in despair. She was on the stage, and she feared she would soon have to give up her profession, and she had no other means of support. She, however, procured a good engagement, and on the opening night, made a great "hit." She received flattering notices from the critics, and was joyful and elated. The next day she received a notice of dismissal. A man in the cast had been jealous of her success and had caused her to be sent away. She felt hatred and resentment taking complete possession of her, and she cried out, "Oh God don't let me hate that man." That night she worked for hours "in the silence."

She said, "I soon came into a very deep silence. I seemed to be at peace with myself, with the man, and with the whole world. I continued this for two following nights, and on the third day I found I was healed completely of the skin disease!" In asking for love, or good-will, she had fulfilled the law, ("for love is the fulfilling of the law") and the disease (which came from subconscious resentment) was wiped out.

Continual criticism produces rheumatism, as critical, inharmonious thoughts cause unnatural deposits in the blood, which settle in the joints.

False growths are caused by jealousy, hatred, unforgiveness, fear, etc. Every disease is caused by a mind not at ease. I said once, in my class, "There is no use asking anyone 'What's the matter with you?' We might just as well say, 'Who's the matter with you?'" Unforgiveness is the most prolific cause of disease. It will harden arteries or liver, and affect the eyesight. In its train are endless ills.

I called on a woman, one day, who said she was ill from having eaten a poisoned oyster. I replied, "Oh, no, the oyster was harmless, you poisoned the oyster. What's the matter with you?" She answered, "Oh about nineteen people." She had quarreled with nineteen people and had become so inharmonious that she attracted the wrong oyster.

Any inharmony on the external, indicates there is mental inharmony. "As the within, so the without."

Man's only enemies are within himself. "And a man's foes shall be they of his own household." Personality is one of the last enemies to be overcome, as this planet is taking its initiation in love. It was Christ's message—"Peace on Earth, good will towards man." The enlightened man, therefore, endeavors to perfect himself upon his neighbor. His work is with himself, to send out goodwill and blessings to every man, and the marvelous thing is, that if one blesses a man he has no power to harm him.

For example: A man came to me asking to "treat" for success in business. He was selling machinery, and a rival appeared on the scene with what he proclaimed, was a better machine, and my friend feared defeat. I said, "First of all, we must wipe out all fear, and know that God protects your interests, and that the divine idea must come out of the situation. That is, the right machine will be sold, by the right man, to the right man." And I added, "Don't hold one critical thought towards that man. Bless him all day, and be willing not to sell your machine, if it isn't the divine idea." So he went to the meeting, fearless and nonresistant, and blessing the other man. He said the outcome was very remarkable. The other man's machine refused to work, and he sold his without the slightest difficulty. "But I say unto you, love your enemies, bless them that curse you, do good to them that hate you, and pray for them which spitefully use you and persecute you."

Good-will produces a great aura of protection about the one who sends it, and "No weapon that is formed against him shall prosper." In other words, love and good-will destroy the enemies within one's self, therefore, one has no enemies on the external!

"There is peace on earth for him who sends good-will to man!"

4

The Law of Nonresistance

Resist not evil. Be not overcome of evil,
but overcome evil with good.

Nothing on earth can resist an absolutely nonresistant person.

The Chinese say that water is the most powerful element, because it is perfectly nonresistant. It can wear away a rock, and sweep all before it.

Jesus Christ said, "Resist not evil," for He knew in reality, there is no evil, therefore nothing to resist. Evil has come of man's "vain imagination," or a belief in two powers, good and evil.

There is an old legend, that Adam and Eve ate of "Maya the Tree of Illusion," and saw two powers instead of one power, God.

Therefore, evil is a false law man has made for himself, through psychoma or soul sleep. Soul sleep means, that man's soul has been hypnotized by the race belief (of sin, sickness and death, etc.) which is carnal or mortal thought, and his affairs have outpictured his illusions.

We have read in a preceding chapter, that man's soul is his subconscious mind, and whatever he feels deeply, good or bad, is outpictured by that faithful servant. His body and affairs show forth what he has been picturing. The sick man has pictured sickness, the poor man, poverty, the rich man, wealth.

People often say, "Why does a little child attract illness, when it is too young even to know what it means?"

I answer that children are sensitive and receptive to the thoughts of others about them, and often outpicture the fears of their parents.

I heard a metaphysician once say, "If you do not run your subconscious mind yourself, someone else will run it for you."

Mothers often, unconsciously, attract illness and disaster to their children, by continually holding them in thoughts of fear, and watching for symptoms.

For example: A friend asked a woman if her little girl had had the measles. She replied promptly, "Not yet!" This implied that she was expecting the illness, and, therefore, preparing the way for what she did not want for herself and child.

However, the man who is centered and established in right thinking, the man who sends out only good-will to his fellow-man, and who is without fear, cannot be *touched or influenced by the negative thoughts of others*. In fact, he could then receive only good thoughts, as he himself, sends forth only good thoughts.

Resistance is Hell, for it places man in a "state of torment."

A metaphysician once gave me a wonderful recipe for taking every trick in the game of life, it is the acme of nonresistance. He gave it in this way: "At one time in my life, I baptized children, and of course, they had many names. Now I no longer baptize children, but I baptize events, but *I give every event the same name*. If I have a failure I baptize it success, in the name of the Father, and of the Son, and of the Holy Ghost!"

In this, we see the great law of transmutation, founded on nonresistance. Through his spoken word, every failure was transmuted into success.

For example: A woman who required money, and who knew the spiritual law of opulence, was thrown continually in a business-way, with a man who made her feel very poor. He talked lack and limitation and she commenced to catch his poverty thoughts, so she disliked him, and blamed him for her failure. She knew in order to demonstrate her supply, she must first feel that she had received—*a feeling of opulence must precede its manifestation.*

It dawned upon her, one day, that she was resisting the situation, and seeing two powers instead of one. So she blessed the man and baptized the situation "Success"! She affirmed, "As there is only one power, God, this man is here for my good and my prosperity" (just what he did not seem to be there for). Soon after that she met, *through this man*, a woman who gave her for a service rendered, several thousand dollars, and the man moved to a distant city, and faded harmoniously from her life. Make the statement, "Every man is a golden link in the chain of my good," for all men are God in manifestation, *awaiting the opportunity given by man, himself, to serve the divine plan of his life.*

"Bless your enemy, and you rob him of his ammunition." His arrows will be transmuted into blessings.

This law is true of nations as well as individuals. Bless a nation, send love and good-will to every inhabitant, and it is robbed of its power to harm.

Man can only get the right idea of nonresistance, through spiritual understanding. My students have often said: "I don't want to be a door-mat." I reply "when you use nonresistance with wisdom, no one will ever be able to walk over you."

Another example: One day I was impatiently awaiting an important telephone call. I resisted every call that came in and made no out-going calls myself, reasoning that it might interfere with the one I was awaiting.

Instead of saying, "Divine ideas never conflict, the call will come at the right time," leaving it to Infinite Intelligence to arrange, I commenced to manage things myself—I made the battle mine, not God's and remained tense and anxious. The bell did not ring for about an hour, and I glanced at the 'phone and found the receiver had been off that length of time, and the 'phone was disconnected. My anxiety, fear and belief in interference, had brought on a total eclipse of the telephone. Realizing what I had done, I commenced blessing the situation at once; I baptized it "success," and affirmed, "I cannot lose any call that belongs to me by divine right; I am under grace, and not under law."

A friend rushed out to the nearest telephone, to notify the Company to reconnect.

She entered a crowded grocery, but the proprietor left his customers and attended to the call himself. My 'phone was connected at once, and two minutes later, I received a very important call, and about an hour afterward, the one I had been awaiting.

One's ships come in over a calm sea.

So long as man resists a situation, he will have it with him. If he runs away from it, it will run after him.

For example: I repeated this to a woman one day, and she replied, "How true that is! I was unhappy at home, I disliked my mother, who was critical and domineering; so I ran away and was married—but I married my mother, for my husband was exactly like my mother, and I had the same situation to face again."

"Agree with thine adversary quickly."

That means, agree that the adverse situation is good, be undisturbed by it, and it falls away of its own weight. "None of these things move me," is a wonderful affirmation.

The inharmonious situation comes from some inharmony within man himself.

When there is, in him, no emotional response to an inharmonious situation, it fades away forever, from his pathway.

So we see man's work is ever with himself.

People have said to me, "Give treatments to change my husband, or my brother." I reply, "No, I will give *treatments to change you*; when you change, your husband and your brother will change."

One of my students was in the habit of lying. I told her it was a failure method and if she lied, she would be lied to. She replied, "I don't care, I can't possibly get along without lying."

One day she was speaking on the 'phone to a man with whom she was very much in love. She turned to me and said, "I don't trust him, I know he's lying to me." I replied, "Well, you lie yourself, so someone has to lie to you, and you will be sure it will be just the person you want the truth from." Some time after that, I saw her, and she said, "I'm cured of lying."

I questioned: "What cured you?"

She replied: "I have been living with a woman who lied worse than I did!"

One is often cured of his faults by seeing them in others.

Life is a mirror, and we find only ourselves reflected in our associates.

Living in the past is a failure method and a violation of spiritual law.

Jesus Christ said, "Behold, now is the accepted time." "Now is the day of Salvation."

Lot's wife looked back and was turned into a pillar of salt.

The robbers of time are the past and the future. Man should bless the past, and forget it, if it keeps him in bondage, and bless the future, knowing it has in store for him endless joys, but live *fully in the now*.

For example: A woman came to me, complaining that she had no money with which to buy Christmas gifts. She said, "Last year was so different; I had plenty of money and gave lovely presents, and this year I have scarcely a cent."

I replied, "You will never demonstrate money while you are pathetic and live in the past. Live fully in the *now*, and *get ready to give Christmas presents*. Dig your ditches, and the money will come." She exclaimed, "I know what to do! I will buy some tinsel twine, Christmas seals and wrapping paper." I replied, "Do that, and the *presents will come and stick themselves to the Christmas seals*."

This too, was showing financial fearlessness and faith in God, as the reasoning mind said, "Keep every cent you have, as you are not sure you will get any more."

She bought the seals, paper and twine, and a few days before Christmas, received a gift of several hundred dollars. Buying the seals and twine had impressed the subconscious with expectancy, and opened the way for the manifestation of the money. She purchased all the presents in plenty of time.

Man must live suspended in the moment.

"Look well, therefore, to this Day! Such is the salutation of the Dawn."

He must be spiritually alert, ever awaiting his leads, taking advantage of every opportunity.

One day, I said continually (silently), "Infinite Spirit, don't let me miss a trick," and something very important was told to me that evening. It is most necessary to begin the day with right words.

Make an affirmation immediately upon waking.

For example:

"*Thy will be done this day! Today is a day of completion; I give thanks for this perfect day, miracle shall follow miracle and wonders shall never cease.*"

Make this a habit, and one will see wonders and miracles come into his life.

One morning I picked up a book and read, "Look with wonder at that which is before you!" It seemed to be my message for the day, so I repeated again and again, "Look with wonder at that which is before you."

At about noon, a large sum of money, was given me, which I had been desiring for a certain purpose.

In a following chapter, I will give affirmations that I have found most effective. However, one should never use an affirmation unless it is absolutely satisfying and convincing to his own consciousness, and often an affirmative is changed to suit different people.

For example: The following has brought success to many:

"I have a wonderful work, in a wonderful way, I give wonderful service, for wonderful pay!"

I gave the first two lines to one of my students, and she added the last two.

It made *a most powerful statement*, as there should always be perfect payment for perfect service, and a rhyme sinks easily into the subconscious. She went about singing it aloud and soon did receive wonderful work in a wonderful way, and gave wonderful service for wonderful pay.

Another student, a business man, took it, and changed the word work to business.

He repeated, "I have a wonderful business, in a wonderful way, and I give wonderful service for wonderful pay." That afternoon he made a forty-one-thousand dollar deal, though there had been no activity in his affairs for months.

Every affirmation must be carefully worded and completely "cover the ground."

For example: I knew a woman, who was in great need, and made a demand for work. She received a great deal of work, but was never paid anything. She now knows to add, "wonderful service for wonderful pay."

It is man's divine right to have plenty! More than enough!

"His barns should be full, and his cup should flow over!" This is God's idea for man, and when man breaks down the barriers of lack in his own consciousness, the Golden Age will be his, and every righteous desire of his heart fulfilled.

5

The Law of Karma and the Law of Forgiveness

Man receives only that which he gives. The Game of Life is a game of boomerangs. Man's thoughts, deeds and words, return to him sooner or later, with astounding accuracy.

This is the law of Karma, which is Sanskrit for "Comeback." "Whatsoever a man soweth, that shall he also reap."

For example: A friend told me this story of herself, illustrating the law. She said, "I make all my Karma on my aunt, whatever I say to her, someone says to me. I am often irritable at home, and one day, said to my aunt, who was talking to me during dinner. *'No more talk, I wish to eat in peace.'*"

"The following day, I was lunching with a woman with whom I wished to make a great impression. I was talking animatedly, when she said: *'No more talk, I wish to eat in peace!'*"

My friend is high in consciousness, so her Karma returns much more quickly than to one on the mental plane.

The more man knows, the more he is responsible for, and a person with a knowledge of Spiritual Law, which he does not practice, suffers greatly, in consequence. "The fear of the Lord (law) is the beginning of wisdom." If we read the word Lord, law, it will make many passages in the Bible much clearer.

"Vengeance is mine, I will repay, saith the Lord" (law). It is the law which takes vengeance, not God. God sees man perfect, "created in his own image," (imagination) and given "power and dominion."

This is the perfect idea of man, registered in Divine Mind, awaiting man's recognition; for man can only be what he sees himself to be, and only attain what he sees himself attaining.

"Nothing ever happens without an on-looker" is an ancient saying.

Man sees first his failure or success, his joy or sorrow, before it swings into visibility from the scenes set in his own imagination. We have observed this in the mother picturing disease for her child, or a woman seeing success for her husband.

Jesus Christ said, "And ye shall know the truth and the truth shall make you free."

So, we see freedom (from all unhappy conditions) comes through knowledge—a knowledge of Spiritual Law.

Obedience precedes authority, and the law obeys man when he obeys the law. The law of electricity must be obeyed before it becomes man's servant. When handled ignorantly, it becomes man's deadly foe. *So with the laws of Mind!*

For example: A woman with a strong personal will, wished she owned a house which belonged to an acquaintance, and she often made mental pictures of herself living in the house. In the course of time, the man died and she moved into the house. Several years afterwards, coming into the knowledge of Spiritual Law, she said to me: "Do you think I had anything to do with that man's death?" I replied: "Yes, your desire was so strong, everything made way for it, but you paid your Karmic debt. Your husband, whom you loved devotedly, died soon after, and the house was a white elephant on your hands for years."

The original owner, however, could not have been affected by her thoughts had he been positive in the truth, nor her husband, but they were both under Karmic law. The woman should have said (feeling the great desire for the house), "Infinite Intelligence, give me the right house, equally as charming as this, the house *which is mine by divine right.*"

The divine selection would have given perfect satisfaction and brought good to all. The divine pattern is the only safe pattern to work by.

Desire is a tremendous force, and must be directed in the right channels, or chaos ensues.

In demonstrating, the most important step is the *first step*, to "*ask aright.*"

Man should always demand only that which is his by *divine right.*

To go back to the illustration: Had the woman taken this attitude: "If this house, I desire, is mine, I cannot lose it, if it is not, give me its equivalent," the man might have decided to move out, harmoniously (had it been the divine selection for her) or another house would have been substituted. Anything forced into manifestation through personal will, is always "ill-got," and has "ever bad success."

Man is admonished, "My will be done not thine," and the curious thing is, man always gets just what he desires when he does relinquish personal will, thereby enabling Infinite Intelligence to work through him.

"Stand ye still and see the salvation of the Lord" (law).

For example: A woman came to me in great distress. Her daughter had determined to take a very hazardous trip, and the mother was filled with fear.

She said she had used every argument, had pointed out the dangers to be encountered, and forbidden her to go, but the daughter became more and more rebellious and determined. I said to the mother, "You are forcing your personal will upon your daughter, which you have no right to do, and your fear of the trip is only attracting it, for man attracts what he fears." I added, "Let go, and take your mental hands off; *put it in God's Hands, and use this statement*: 'I put this situation in the hands of Infinite Love and Wisdom; if this trip is the Divine plan, I bless it and no longer resist, but if it is not divinely planned, I give thanks that it is now dissolved and dissipated.'" A day or two after that, her daughter said to her, "Mother, I have given up the trip," and the situation returned to its "native nothingness."

It is learning to "stand still," which seems so difficult for man. I will deal more fully with this law in the chapter on nonresistance.

I will give another example of sowing and reaping, which came in the most curious way.

A woman came to me saying, she had received a counterfeit twenty-dollar bill, given to her at the bank. She was much disturbed, for, she said, "The people at the bank will never acknowledge their mistake."

I replied, "Let us analyze the situation and find out why you attracted it." She thought a few moments and exclaimed: "I know it, I sent a friend a lot of stage money, just for a joke." So the law had sent her some stage money, for it doesn't know anything about jokes.

I said, "Now we will call on the law of forgiveness, and neutralize the situation."

Christianity is founded upon the law of forgiveness—Christ has redeemed us from the curse of the Karmic law, and the Christ within each man is his Redeemer and Salvation from all inharmonious conditions.

So I said: "Infinite Spirit, we call on the law of forgiveness and give thanks that she is under grace and not under law, and cannot lose this twenty dollars which is hers by divine right."

"Now," I said, "Go back to the bank and tell them, fearlessly, that it was given you, there by mistake."

She obeyed, and to her surprise, they apologized and gave her another bill, treating her most courteously.

So knowledge of the Law gives man power to "rub out his mistakes." Man cannot force the external to be what he is not.

If he desires riches, he must be rich first in consciousness.

For example: A woman came to me asking treatment for prosperity. She did not take much interest in her household affairs, and her home was in great disorder.

I said to her, "If you wish to be rich, you must be orderly. All men with great wealth are orderly—and order is heaven's first law." I added, "You will never become rich with a burnt match in the pincushion."

She had a good sense of humor and commenced immediately, putting her house in order. She rearranged furniture, straightened out bureau drawers, cleaned rugs, and soon made a big financial demonstration—a gift from a relative. The woman, herself, became made over, and keeps herself keyed-up financially, by being ever watchful of the *external and expecting prosperity, knowing God is her supply*.

Many people are in ignorance of the fact that gifts and things are investments, and that hoarding and saving invariably lead to loss.

"There is that scattereth and yet increaseth; and there is that withholdeth more than is meet, but it tendeth to poverty."

For example: I knew a man who wanted to buy a fur-lined overcoat. He and his wife went to various shops, but there was none he wanted. He said they were all too cheap-looking. At last, he was shown one, the salesman said was valued at a thousand dollars, but which the manager would sell him for five-hundred dollars, as it was late in the season.

His financial possessions amounted to about seven hundred dollars. The reasoning mind would have said, "You can't afford to spend nearly all you have on a coat," but he was very intuitive and never reasoned.

He turned to his wife and said, "If I get this coat, I'll make a ton of money!" So his wife consented, weakly.

About a month later, he received a ten-thousand-dollar commission. The coat made him feel so rich, it linked him with success and prosperity; without the coat, he would not have received the commission. It was an investment paying large dividends!

If man ignores these leadings to spend or to give, the same amount of money will go in an uninteresting or unhappy way.

For example: A woman told me, on Thanksgiving Day, she informed her family that they could not afford a Thanksgiving dinner. She had the money, but decided to save it.

A few days later, someone entered her room and took from the bureau drawer the exact amount the dinner would have cost.

The law always stands back of the man who spends fearlessly, with wisdom.

For example: One of my students was shopping with her little nephew. The child clamored for a toy, which she told him she could not afford to buy.

She realized suddenly that she was seeking lack, and not recognizing God as her supply!

So she bought the toy, and on her way home, *picked up, in the street, the exact amount of money she had paid for it.*

Man's supply is inexhaustible and unfailing when fully trusted, but faith or trust must precede the demonstration. "According to your faith be it unto you." "Faith is the substance of things hoped for, the evidence of things not seen—" for faith holds the vision steady, and the adverse pictures are dissolved and dissipated, and "in due season we shall reap, if we faint not."

Jesus Christ brought the good news (the gospel) that there was a higher law than the law of Karma—and that that law transcends the law of Karma. It is the law of grace, or forgiveness. It is the law which *frees man from the law of cause and effect—the law of consequence. "Under grace, and not under law."*

We are told that on this plane, man reaps where he has not sown; the gifts of God are simply poured out upon him. "All that the Kingdom affords is his." This continued state of bliss awaits the man who has overcome the race (or world) thought.

In the world thought there is tribulation, but Jesus Christ said: "Be of good cheer; I have overcome the world."

The world thought is that of sin, sickness and death. He saw their absolute unreality and said sickness and sorrow shall pass away and death itself, the last enemy, be overcome.

We know now, from a scientific standpoint, that death could be overcome by stamping the subconscious mind with the conviction of eternal youth and eternal life.

The subconscious, being simply power without direction, *carries out orders without questioning.*

Working under the direction of the superconscious (the Christ or God within man) the "resurrection of the body" would be accomplished.

Man would no longer throw off his body in death, it would be transformed into the "body electric," sung by Walt Whitman, for Christianity is founded upon the forgiveness of sins and "an empty tomb."

6

CASTING THE BURDEN
(IMPRESSING THE SUBCONSCIOUS)

When man knows his own powers and the workings of his mind, his great desire is to find an easy and quick way to impress the subconscious with good, for simply an intellectual knowledge of the Truth will not bring results.

In my own case, I found the easiest way is in "casting the burden."

A metaphysician once explained it in this manner. He said, "The only thing which gives anything weight in nature, is the law of gravitation, and if a boulder could be taken high above the planet, there would be no weight in that boulder; and that is what Jesus Christ meant when he said: 'My yoke is easy and my burden is light.'"

He had overcome the world vibration, and functioned in the fourth dimensional realm, where there is only perfection, completion, life and joy.

He said: "Come to me all ye that labor and are heavy laden, and I will give you rest." "Take my yoke upon you, for my yoke is easy and my burden is light."

We are also told in the fifty-fifth Psalm, to "cast thy burden upon the Lord." Many passages in the Bible state that the *battle is God's* not man's and that man is always to *"stand still" and see the Salvation of the Lord.*

This indicates that the superconscious mind (or Christ within) is the department which fights man's battle and relieves him of burdens.

We see, therefore, that man violates law if he carries a burden, and a burden is an adverse thought or condition, and this thought or condition has its root in the subconscious.

It seems almost impossible to make any headway directing the subconscious from the conscious, or reasoning mind, as the reasoning mind (the intellect) is limited in its conceptions, and filled with doubts and fears.

How scientific it then is, to cast the burden upon the super-conscious mind (or Christ within) where it is "made light," or dissolved into its "native nothingness."

For example: A woman in urgent need of money, "made light" upon the Christ within, the superconscious, with the statement, "I cast this burden of lack on the Christ (within) and I go free to have plenty!"

The belief in lack was her burden, and as she cast it upon the Superconscious with its belief of plenty, an avalanche of supply was the result.

We read, "The Christ in you the hope of glory."

Another example: One of my students had been given a new piano, and there was no room in her studio for it until she had moved out the old one. She was in a state of perplexity. She wanted to keep the old piano, but knew of no place to send it. She became desperate, as the new piano was to be sent immediately; in fact, was on its way, with no place to put it. She said it came to her to repeat, "I cast this burden on the Christ within, and I go free."

A few moments later, her 'phone rang, and a woman friend asked if she might rent her old piano, and it was moved out, a few minutes before the new one arrived.

I knew a woman, whose burden was resentment. She said, "I cast this burden of resentment on the Christ within, and I go free, to be loving, harmonious and happy." The Almighty super-conscious, flooded the subconscious with love, and her whole life was changed. For years, resentment had held her in a state of torment and imprisoned her soul (the subconscious mind).

The statement should be made over and over and over, some-times for hours at a time, silently or audibly, with quietness but determination.

I have often compared it to winding-up a victrola. We must wind ourselves up with spoken words.

I have noticed, in "casting the burden," after a little while, one seems to see clearly. It is impossible to have clear vision, while in the throes of carnal mind. Doubts and fear poison the mind and body and imagination runs riot, attracting disaster and disease.

In steadily repeating the affirmation, "I cast this burden on the Christ within, and go free," the vision clears, and with it a feeling of relief, and sooner or later comes *the manifestation of good, be it health, happiness or supply*.

One of my students once asked me to explain the "darkness before the dawn." I referred in a preceding chapter to the fact that often, before the big demonstration "everything seems to go wrong," and deep depression clouds the consciousness. It means that out of the subconscious are rising the doubts and fears of the ages. These old derelicts of the subconscious rise to the surface, to be put out.

It is then, that man should clap his cymbals, like Jehoshaphat, and give thanks that he is saved, even though he seems sur-rounded by the enemy (the situation of lack or disease). The student continued, "How long must one remain in the dark" and

I replied, "*until one can see in the dark*," and "*casting the burden enables one to see in the dark*."

In order to impress the subconscious, active faith is always essential.

"Faith without works is dead." In these chapters I have endeavored to bring out this point.

Jesus Christ showed active faith when "He commanded the multitude to sit down on the ground," before he gave thanks for the loaves and the fishes.

I will give another example showing how necessary this step is. In fact, active faith is the bridge, over which man passes to his Promised Land.

Through misunderstanding, a woman had been separated from her husband, whom she loved deeply. He refused all offers of reconciliation and would not communicate with her in any way.

Coming into the knowledge of Spiritual law, she denied the appearance of separation. She made this statement: "There is no separation in Divine Mind, therefore, I cannot be separated from the love and companionship which are mine by divine right."

She showed active faith by arranging a place for him at the table every day; thereby impressing the subconscious with a picture of his *return*. Over a year passed, but she never wavered, and *one day he walked in*.

The subconscious is often impressed through music. Music has a fourth dimensional quality and releases the soul from imprisonment. It makes wonderful things seem *possible, and easy of accomplishment*!

I have a friend who uses her victrola, daily, for this purpose. It puts her in perfect harmony and releases the imagination.

Another woman often dances while making her affirmations. The rhythm and harmony of music and motion carry her words forth with tremendous power.

The student must remember also, not to despise the "day of small things."

Invariably, before a demonstration, come "signs of land."

Before Columbus reached America, he saw birds and twigs which showed him land was near. So it is with a demonstration; but often the student mistakes it for the demonstration itself, and is disappointed.

For example: A woman had "spoken the word" for a set of dishes. Not long afterwards a friend gave her a dish which was old and cracked.

She came to me and said, "Well, I asked for a set of dishes, and all I got was a cracked plate."

I replied, "The plate was only signs of land. It shows your dishes are coming—look upon it as birds and seaweed," and not long afterwards the dishes came.

Continually "making-believe," impresses the subconscious. If one makes believe he is rich, and makes believe he is successful, in "due time he will reap."

Children are always "making believe," and "except ye be converted, and become as little children, ye shall not enter the Kingdom of Heaven."

For example: I know of a woman who was very poor, but no one could make her *feel poor*. She earned a small amount of money from rich friends, who constantly reminded her of her poverty, and to be careful and saving. Regardless of their admonitions, she would spend all her earnings on a hat, or make someone a gift, and be in a rapturous state of mind. Her thoughts were always centered on beautiful clothes and "rings and things," but without envying others.

She lived in the world of the wondrous, and only riches seemed real to her. Before long she married a rich man, and the rings and things became visible. I do not know whether the man was the "Divine Selection," but opulence had to manifest in her life, as she had imagined only opulence.

There is no peace or happiness for man, until he has erased all fear from the subconscious.

Fear is misdirected energy and must be redirected, or transmuted into Faith.

Jesus Christ said, "Why are ye fearful, O ye of little faith?" "All things are possible to him that believeth."

I am asked, so often by my students, "*How can I get rid of fear?*"

I reply, "By *walking up to the thing you are afraid of.*"

"The lion takes its fierceness from your fear."

Walk up to the lion, and he will disappear; run away and he runs after you.

I have shown in previous chapters, how the lion of lack disappeared when the individual spent money fearlessly, showing faith that God was his supply and therefore, unfailing.

Many of my students have come out of the bondage of poverty, and are now bountifully supplied, through losing all fear of letting money go out. The subconscious is impressed with the truth that *God is the Giver and the Gift*; therefore as one is one with the Giver, he is one with the Gift. A splendid statement is, "I now thank God the Giver for God the Gift."

Man has so long separated himself from his good and his supply, through thoughts of separation and lack, that sometimes, it takes dynamite to dislodge these false ideas from the subconscious, and the dynamite is a big situation.

We see in the foregoing illustration, how the individual was freed from his bondage by *showing fearlessness.*

Man should watch himself hourly to detect if his motive for action is fear or faith.

"Choose ye this day whom we shall serve," fear or faith.

Perhaps one's fear is of personality. Then do not avoid the people feared; be willing to meet them cheerfully, and they will either prove "golden links in the chain of one's good," or disappear harmoniously from one's pathway.

Perhaps one's fear is of disease or germs. Then one should be fearless and undisturbed in a germ-laden situation, and he would be immune.

One can only contract germs while vibrating at the same rate as the germ, and fear drags men down to the level of the germ. Of course, the disease-laden germ is the product of carnal mind, as all thought must objectify. Germs do not exist in the superconscious or Divine Mind, therefore are the product of man's "vain imagination."

"In the twinkling of an eye," man's release will come when he realizes *there is no power in evil.*

The material world will fade away, and the fourth dimensional world, the "World of the Wondrous," will swing into manifestation.

"And I saw a new heaven, and a new earth—and there shall be no more death, neither sorrow nor crying, neither shall there be any more pain; for the former things are passed away."

7

LOVE

Every man on this planet is taking his initiation in love. "A new commandment I give unto you, that ye love one another." Ouspensky states, in "Tertium Organum," that "love is a cosmic phenomenon," and opens to man the fourth dimensional world, "The World of the Wondrous."

Real love is selfless and free from fear. It pours itself out upon the object of its affection, without demanding any return. Its joy is in the joy of giving. Love is God in manifestation, and the strongest magnetic force in the universe. Pure, unselfish love *draws to itself its own*; it does not need to seek or demand. Scarcely anyone has the faintest conception of real love. Man is selfish, tyrannical or fearful in his affections, thereby losing the thing he loves. Jealousy is the worst enemy of love, for the imagination runs riot, seeing the loved one attracted to another, and invariably these fears objectify if they are not neutralized.

For example: A woman came to me in deep distress. The man she loved had left her for other women, and said he never intended to marry her. She was torn with jealousy and resentment and said she hoped he would suffer as he had made her suffer; and added, "How could he leave me when I loved him so much?"

I replied, "You are not loving that man, you are hating him," and added, "*You can never receive what you have never given. Give a perfect love and you will receive a perfect love.* Perfect yourself on this man. Give him a perfect, *unselfish* love, demanding nothing in return, do not criticize or condemn, and *bless him wherever he is.*"

She replied, "No, I won't bless him unless I know where he is!"

"Well," I said, "that is not real love."

"When you *send out real love*, real love will return to you, either from this man or his equivalent, for if this man is not the divine selection, you will not want him. As you are one with God, you are one with the love which belongs to you by divine right."

Several months passed, and matters remained about the same, but she was working conscientiously with herself. I said, "When you are no longer disturbed by his cruelty, he will cease to be cruel, as you are attracting it through your own emotions."

Then I told her of a brotherhood in India, who never said, "Good morning" to each other. They used these words: "*I salute the Divinity in you.*" They saluted the divinity in every man, and in the wild animals in the jungle, and they were never harmed, for they *saw only God in every* living thing. I said, "Salute the divinity in this man, and say, 'I see your divine self only. I see you as God sees you, perfect, made in His image and likeness.'"

She found she was becoming more poised, and gradually losing her resentment. He was a Captain, and she always called him "The Cap."

One day, she said, suddenly, "*God bless the Cap wherever he is.*"

I replied: "Now, that is real love, and when you have become a 'complete circle,' and are no longer disturbed by the situation, you will have his love, or attract its equivalent."

I was moving at this time, and did not have a telephone, so was out of touch with her for a few weeks, when one morning I received a letter saying, "We are married."

At the earliest opportunity, I paid her a call. My first words were, "What happened?"

"Oh," she exclaimed, "a miracle! One day I woke up and all suffering had ceased. I saw him that evening and he asked me to marry him. We were married in about a week, and I have never seen a more devoted man."

There is an old saying: "*No man is your enemy, no man is your friend, every man is your teacher.*"

So one should become impersonal and learn what each man has to teach him, and soon he would learn his lessons and be free.

The woman's lover was teaching her selfless love, which every man, sooner or later, must learn.

Suffering is not necessary for man's development; it is the result of violation of spiritual law, but few people seem able to rouse themselves from their "soul sleep" without it. When people are happy, they usually become selfish, and automatically the law of Karma is set in action. Man often suffers loss through lack of appreciation.

I knew a woman who had a very nice husband, but she said often, "I don't care anything about being married, but that is nothing against my husband. I'm simply not interested in married life."

She had other interests, and scarcely remembered she had a husband. She only thought of him when she saw him. One day her husband told her he was in love with another woman, and left. She came to me in distress and resentment.

I replied, "It is exactly what you spoke the word for. You said you didn't care anything about being married, so the subconscious worked to get you unmarried."

She said, "Oh yes, I see. People get what they want, and then feel very much hurt."

She soon became in perfect harmony with the situation, and knew they were both much happier apart.

When a woman becomes indifferent or critical, and ceases to be an inspiration to her husband, he misses the stimulus of their early relationship and is restless and unhappy.

A man came to me dejected, miserable and poor. His wife was interested in the "Science of Numbers," and had had him read. It seems the report was not very favorable, for he said, "My wife says I'll never amount to anything because I am a two."

I replied, "I don't care what your number is, you are a perfect idea in divine mind, and we will demand the success and prosperity which are *already planned* for you by that Infinite Intelligence."

Within a few weeks, he had a very fine position, and a year or two later, he achieved a brilliant success as a writer. No man is a success in business unless he loves his work. The picture the artist paints for love (of his art) is his greatest work. The pot-boiler is always something to live down.

No man can attract money if he despises it. Many people are kept in poverty by saying: "Money means nothing to me, and I have a contempt for people who have it."

This is the reason so many artists are poor. Their contempt for money separates them from it.

I remember hearing one artist say of another, "He's no good as an artist, he has money in the bank."

This attitude of mind, of course, separates man from his supply; he must be in harmony with a thing in order to attract it.

Money is God in manifestation, as freedom from want and limitation, but it must be always kept in circulation and put to right uses. Hoarding and saving react with grim vengeance.

This does not mean that man should not have houses and lots, stocks and bonds, for "the barns of the righteous man shall be full." It means man should not hoard even the principal, if an occasion arises, when money is necessary. In letting it go out fearlessly and cheerfully he opens the way for more to come in, for God is man's unfailing and inexhaustible supply.

This is the spiritual attitude towards money and the great Bank of the Universal never fails!

We see an example of hoarding in the film production of "Greed." The woman won five thousand dollars in a lottery, but would not spend it. She hoarded and saved, let her husband suffer and starve, and eventually she scrubbed floors for a living.

She loved the money itself and put it above everything, and one night she was murdered and the money taken from her.

This is an example of where "love of money is the root of all evil." Money in itself, is good and beneficial, but used for destructive purposes, hoarded and saved, or considered more important than love, brings disease and disaster, and the loss of the money itself.

Follow the path of love, and all things are added, *for God is love*, and *God is supply*; follow the path of selfishness and greed, and the supply vanishes, or man is separated from it.

For example; I knew the case of a very rich woman, who hoarded her income. She rarely gave anything away, but bought and bought and bought things for herself.

She was very fond of necklaces, and a friend once asked her how many she possessed. She replied, "Sixty-seven." She bought them and put them away, carefully wrapped in tissue paper. Had she used the necklaces it would have been quite legitimate, but she was violating "the law of use." Her closets were filled with clothes she never wore, and jewels which never saw the light.

The woman's arms were gradually becoming paralyzed from holding on to things, and eventually she was considered incapable of looking after her affairs and her wealth was handed over to others to manage.

So man, in ignorance of the law, brings about his own destruction.

All disease, all unhappiness, come from the violation of the law of love. Man's boomerangs of hate, resentment and criticism, come back laden with sickness and sorrow. Love seems almost a lost art, but the man with the knowledge of spiritual law knows it must be regained, for without it, he has "become as sounding brass and tinkling cymbals."

For example: I had a student who came to me, month after month, to clean her consciousness of resentment. After a while, she arrived at the point where she resented only one woman, but that one woman kept her busy. Little by little she became poised and harmonious, and one day, all resentment was wiped out.

She came in radiant, and exclaimed "You can't understand how I feel! The woman said something to me and instead of being furious I was loving and kind, and she apologized and was perfectly lovely to me.

"No one can understand the marvelous lightness I feel within!"

Love and good-will are invaluable in business. For example: A woman came to me, complaining of her employer. She said she was cold and critical and knew she did not want her in the position.

"Well," I replied, "Salute the Divinity in the woman and send her love."

She said "I can't; she's a marble woman."

I answered, "You remember the story of the sculptor who asked for a certain piece of marble. He was asked why he wanted it, and he replied, 'because there is an angel in the marble,' and out of it he produced a wonderful work of art."

She said, "Very well, I'll try it." A week later she came back and said, "I did what you told me to, and now the woman is very kind, and took me out in her car."

People are sometimes filled with remorse for having done someone an unkindness, perhaps years ago.

If the wrong cannot be righted, its effect can be neutralized by doing some one a kindness *in the present.*

"This one thing I do, forgetting those things which are behind and reaching forth unto those things which are before."

Sorrow, regret and remorse tear down the cells of the body, and poison the atmosphere of the individual.

A woman said to me in deep sorrow, "Treat me to be happy and joyous, for my sorrow makes me so irritable with the members of my family that I keep making more Karma."

I was asked to treat a woman who was mourning for her daughter. I denied all belief in loss and separation, and affirmed that God was the woman's joy, love and peace.

The woman gained her poise at once, but sent word by her son, not to treat any longer, because she was "so happy, it wasn't respectable."

So "mortal mind" loves to hang on to its griefs and regrets.

I knew a woman who went about bragging of her troubles, so, of course, she always had something to brag about.

The old idea was if a woman did not worry about her children, she was not a good mother.

Now, we know that mother-fear is responsible for many of the diseases and accidents which come into the lives of children.

For fear pictures vividly the disease or situation feared, and these pictures objectify, if not neutralized.

Happy is the mother who can say sincerely, that she puts her child in God's hands, and knows therefore, that he is divinely protected.

For example: A woman awoke suddenly, in the night, feeling her brother was in great danger. Instead of giving in to her fears, she commenced making statements of Truth, saying, "Man is a perfect idea in Divine Mind, and is always in his right place, therefore, my brother is in his right place, and is divinely protected."

The next day she found that her brother had been in close proximity to an explosion in a mine, but had miraculously escaped.

So man is his brother's keeper (in thought) and every man should know that the thing he loves dwells in "the secret place of the most high, and abides under the shadow of the Almighty."

"There shall no evil befall thee, neither shall any plague come nigh thy dwelling."

"Perfect love casteth out fear. He that feareth is not made perfect in love," and "Love is the fulfilling of the Law."

8

INTUITION OR GUIDANCE

In all thy ways acknowledge Him and
He shall direct thy paths.

There is nothing too great of accomplishment for the man who knows the power of his word, and who follows his intuitive leads. By the word he starts in action unseen forces and can rebuild his body or remold his affairs.

It is, therefore, of the utmost importance to choose the right words, and the student carefully selects the affirmation he wishes to catapult into the invisible.

He knows that God is his supply, that there is a supply for every demand, and that his spoken word releases this supply.

"Ask and ye shall receive."

Man must make the first move. "Draw nigh to God and He will draw nigh to you."

I have often been asked just how to make a demonstration.

I reply: "Speak the word and then do not do anything until you get a definite lead." Demand the lead, saying, "Infinite Spirit, reveal to me the way, let me know if there is anything for me to do."

The answer will come through intuition (or hunch); a chance remark from someone, or a passage in a book, etc., etc. The answers are sometimes quite startling in their exactness. For example: A woman desired a large sum of money. She spoke the words: "Infinite Spirit, open the way for my immediate supply, let all that is mine by divine right now reach me, in great avalanches of abundance." Then she added: "Give me a definite lead, let me know if there is anything for me to do."

The thought came quickly, "Give a certain friend" (who had helped her spiritually) "a hundred dollars." She told her friend, who said, "Wait and get another lead, before giving it." So she waited, and that day met a woman who said to her, "I gave someone a dollar today; it was just as much for me, as it would be for you to give someone a hundred."

This was indeed an unmistakable lead, so she knew she was right in giving the hundred dollars. It was a gift which proved a great investment, for shortly after that, a large sum of money came to her in a remarkable way.

Giving opens the way for receiving. In order to create activity in finances, one should give. Tithing or giving one-tenth of one's income, is an old Jewish custom, and is sure to bring increase. Many of the richest men in this country have been tithers, and I have never known it to fail as an investment.

The tenth-part goes forth and returns blessed and multiplied. But the gift or tithe must be given with love and cheerfulness, for "God loveth a cheerful giver." Bills should be paid cheerfully; all money should be sent forth fearlessly and with a blessing.

This attitude of mind makes man master of money. It is his to obey, and his spoken word then opens vast reservoirs of wealth.

Man, himself, limits his supply by his limited vision. Sometimes the student has a great realization of wealth, but is afraid to act.

The vision and action must go hand in hand, as in the case of the man who bought the fur-lined overcoat.

A woman came to me asking me to "speak the word" for a position. So I demanded: "Infinite Spirit, open the way for this woman's right position." Never ask for just "a position"; ask for the right position, the place already planned in Divine Mind, as it is the only one that will give satisfaction.

I then gave thanks that she had already received, and that it would manifest quickly. Very soon, she had three positions offered her, two in New York and one in Palm Beach, and she did not know which to choose. I said, "Ask for a definite lead."

The time was almost up and was still undecided, when one day, she telephoned, "When I woke up this morning, I could smell Palm Beach." She had been there before and knew its balmy fragrance.

I replied: "Well, if you can smell Palm Beach from here, it is certainly your lead." She accepted the position, and it proved a great success. Often one's lead comes at an unexpected time.

One day, I was walking down the street, when I suddenly felt a strong urge to go to a certain bakery, a block or two away.

The reasoning mind resisted, arguing, "There is nothing there that you want."

However, I had learned not to reason, so I went to the bakery, looked at everything, and there was certainly nothing there that I wanted, but coming out I encountered a woman I had thought of often, and who was in great need of the help which I could give her.

So often, one goes for one thing and finds another.

Intuition is a spiritual faculty and does not explain, but simply points the way.

A person often receives a lead during a "treatment." The idea that comes may seem quite irrelevant, but some of God's leadings are "mysterious."

In the class, one day, I was treating that each individual would receive a definite lead. A woman came to me afterwards, and said: "While you were treating, I got the hunch to take my furniture out of storage and get an apartment." The woman had come to be treated for health. I told her I knew in getting a home of her own, her health would improve, and I added, "I believe your trouble, which is a congestion, has come from having things stored away. Congestion of things causes congestion in the body. You have violated the law of use, and your body is paying the penalty."

So I gave thanks that *"Divine order was established in her mind, body and affairs."*

People little dream of how their affairs react on the body. There is a mental correspondence for every disease. A person might receive instantaneous healing through the realization of his body being a perfect idea in Divine Mind, and, therefore, whole and perfect, but if he continues his destructive thinking, hoarding, hating, fearing, condemning, the disease will return.

Jesus Christ knew that all sickness came from sin, but admonished the leper after the healing, to go and sin no more, lest a worse thing come upon him.

So man's soul (or subconscious mind) must be washed whiter than snow, for permanent healing; and the metaphysician is always delving deep for the "correspondence."

Jesus Christ said, "Condemn not lest ye also be condemned."

"Judge not, lest ye be judged."

Many people have attracted disease and unhappiness through condemnation of others.

What man condemns in others, he attracts to himself.

For example: A friend came to me in anger and distress, because her husband had deserted her for another woman. She condemned the other woman, and said continually, "She knew he was a married man, and had no right to accept his attentions."

I replied. "Stop condemning the woman, bless her, and be through with the situation, otherwise, you are attracting the same thing to yourself."

She was deaf to my words, and a year or two later, became deeply interested in a married man, herself.

Man picks up a live-wire whenever he criticizes or condemns, and may expect a shock.

Indecision is a stumbling-block in many a pathway. In order to overcome it, make the statement, repeatedly, "*I am always under direct inspiration; I make right decisions, quickly.*"

These words impress the subconscious, and soon one finds himself awake and alert, making his right moves without hesitation. I have found it destructive to look to the psychic plane for guidance, as it is the plane of many minds and not "The One Mind."

As man opens his mind to subjectivity, he becomes a target for destructive forces. The psychic plane is the result of man's mortal thought, and is on the "plane of opposites." He may receive either good or bad messages.

The science of numbers and the reading of horoscopes, keep man down on the mental (or mortal) plane, for they deal only with the Karmic path.

I know of a man who should have been dead, years ago, according to his horoscope, but he is alive and a leader of one of the biggest movements in this country for the uplift of humanity.

It takes a very strong mind to neutralize a prophecy of evil. The student should declare, "Every false prophecy shall come to naught; every plan my Father in heaven has not planned, shall be dissolved and dissipated, the divine idea now comes to pass."

However, if any good message has ever been given one, of coming happiness, or wealth, harbor and expect it, and it will manifest sooner or later, through the law of expectancy.

Man's will should be used to back the universal will. "I will that the will of God be done."

It is God's will to give every man, every righteous desire of his heart, and man's will should be used to hold the perfect vision, without wavering.

The prodigal son said: "I will arise and go to my Father."

It is, indeed, often an effort of the will to leave the husks and swine of mortal thinking. It is so much easier, for the average person, to have fear than faith; *so faith is an effort of the will.*

As man becomes spiritually awakened he recognizes that any external inharmony is the correspondence of mental inharmony. If he stumbles or falls, he may know he is stumbling or falling in consciousness.

One day, a student was walking along the street condemning someone in her thoughts. She was saying, mentally, "That woman is the most disagreeable woman on earth," when suddenly three boy scouts rushed around the corner and almost knocked her over. She did not condemn the boy scouts, but immediately called on the law of forgiveness, and "saluted the divinity" in the woman. Wisdom's way are ways of pleasantness and all her paths are peace.

When one has made his demands upon the Universal, he must be ready for surprises. Everything may seem to be going wrong, when in reality, it is going right.

For example: A woman was told that there was no loss in divine mind, therefore, she could not lose anything which belonged to her; anything lost, would be returned, or she would receive its equivalent.

Several years previously, she had lost two thousand dollars. She had loaned the money to a relative during her lifetime, but the relative had died, leaving no mention of it in her will. The woman was resentful and angry, and as she had no written statement of the transaction, she never received the money, so she determined to deny the loss, and collect the two thousand dollars from the Bank of the Universal. She had to begin by forgiving the woman, as resentment and unforgiveness close the doors of this wonderful bank.

She made this statement, "I deny loss, there is no loss in Divine Mind, therefore, I cannot lose the two thousand dollars, which belong to me by divine right. *As one door shuts another door opens.*"

She was living in an apartment house which was for sale; and in the lease was a clause, stating that if the house was sold, the tenants would be required to move out within ninety days.

Suddenly, the landlord broke the leases and raised the rent. Again, injustice was on her pathway, but this time she was undisturbed. She blessed the landlord, and said, "As the rent has been raised, it means that I'll be that much richer, for God is my supply."

New leases were made out for the advanced rent, but by some divine mistake, the ninety days clause had been forgotten. Soon after, the landlord had an opportunity to sell the house. On account of the mistake in the new leases, the tenants held possession for another year.

The agent offered each tenant two hundred dollars if he would vacate. Several families moved; three remained, including the woman. A month or two passed, and the agent again appeared. This time he said to the woman, "Will you break your lease for the sum of fifteen hundred dollars?" It flashed upon her, "Here comes the two thousand dollars." She remembered having said to friends in the house, "We will all act together if anything more is said about leaving." So her *lead* was to consult her friends.

These friends said: "Well, if they have offered you fifteen hundred they will certainly give two thousand." So she received a check for two thousand dollars for giving up the apartment.

It was certainly a remarkable working of the law, and the apparent injustice was merely opening the way for her demonstration.

It proved that there is no loss, and when man takes his spiritual stand, he collects all that is his from this great Reservoir of Good.

"I will restore to you the years the locusts have eaten."

The locusts are the doubts, fears, resentments and regrets of mortal thinking.

These adverse thoughts, alone, rob man; for "No man gives to himself but himself, and no man takes away from himself, but himself."

Man is here to prove God and "to bear witness to the truth," and he can only prove God by bringing plenty out of lack, and justice out of injustice.

"Prove me now herewith, saith the Lord of hosts, if I will not open you the windows of heaven, and pour out a blessing, that there shall not be room enough to receive it."

9

PERFECT SELF-EXPRESSION
OR THE DIVINE DESIGN

No wind can drive my bark astray
nor change the tide of destiny.

There is for each man, perfect self-expression. There is a place which he is to fill and no one else can fill, something which he is to do, which no one else can do; it is his destiny!

This achievement is held, a perfect idea in Divine Mind, awaiting man's recognition. As the imaging faculty is the creative faculty, it is necessary for man to see the idea, before it can manifest.

So man's highest demand is for the *Divine Design of his life.*

He may not have the faintest conception of what it is, for there is, possibly, some marvelous talent, hidden deep within him.

His demand should be: "*Infinite Spirit, open the way for the Divine Design of my life to manifest; let the genius within me now be released; let me see clearly the perfect plan.*"

The perfect plan includes health, wealth, love and perfect self-expression. This is the *square of life*, which brings perfect happiness. When one has made this demand, he may find great changes taking place in his life, for nearly every man has wandered far from the Divine Design.

I know, in one woman's case, it was as though a cyclone had struck her affairs, but readjustments came quickly, and new and wonderful conditions took the place of old ones.

Perfect self-expression will never be labor; but of such absorbing interest that it will seem almost like play. The student knows, also, as man comes into the world financed by God, the *supply* needed for his perfect self-expression will be at hand.

Many a genius has struggled for years with the problem of supply, when his spoken word, and faith, would have released quickly, the necessary funds.

For example: After the class, one day, a man came to me and handed me a cent.

He said: "I have just seven cents in the world, and I'm going to give you one; for I have faith in the power of your spoken word. I want you to speak the word for my perfect self-expression and prosperity."

I "spoke the word," and did not see him again until a year later. He came in one day, successful and happy, with a roll of yellow bills in his pocket. He said, "Immediately after you spoke the word, I had a position offered me in a distant city, and am now demonstrating health, happiness and supply."

A woman's perfect self-expression may be in becoming a perfect wife, a perfect mother, a perfect home-maker and not necessarily in having a public career.

Demand definite leads, and the way will be made easy and successful.

One should not visualize or force a mental picture. When he demands the Divine Design to come into his conscious mind, he will receive flashes of inspiration, and begin to see himself making some great accomplishment. This is the picture, or idea, he must hold without wavering.

The thing man seeks is seeking him—*the telephone was seeking Bell!*

Parents should never force careers and professions upon their children. With a knowledge of spiritual Truth, the Divine Plan could be spoken for, early in childhood, or prenatally.

A prenatal treatment should be: "Let the God in this child have perfect expression; let the Divine Design of his mind, body and affairs be made manifest throughout his life, throughout eternity."

God's will be done, not man's; God's pattern, not man's pattern, is the command we find running through all the scriptures, and the Bible is a book dealing with the science of the mind. It is a book telling man how to release his soul (or subconscious mind) from bondage.

The battles described are pictures of man waging war against mortal thoughts. "A man's foes shall be they of his own household." Every man is Jehoshaphat, and every man is David, who slays Goliath (mortal thinking) with the little white stone (faith).

So man must be careful that he is not the "wicked and slothful servant" who buried his talent. There is a terrible penalty to be paid for not using one's ability.

Often fear stands between man and his perfect self-expression. Stage-fright has hampered many a genius. This may be overcome by the spoken word, or treatment. The individual then loses all self-consciousness, and feels simply that he is a channel for Infinite Intelligence to express Itself through.

He is under direct inspiration, fearless, and confident; for he feels that it is the "Father within" him who does the work.

A young boy came often to my class with his mother. He asked me to "speak the word" for his coming examinations at school.

I told him to make the statement: "I am one with Infinite Intelligence. I know everything I should know on this subject." He had an excellent knowledge of history, but was not sure of his arithmetic. I saw him afterwards, and he said: "I spoke the word for my arithmetic, and passed with the highest honors; but thought I could depend on myself for history, and got a very poor mark." Man often receives a set-back when he is "too sure of himself," which means he is trusting to his personality and not the "Father within."

Another one of my students gave me an example of this. She took an extended trip abroad one summer, visiting many countries, where she was ignorant of the languages. She was calling for guidance and protection every minute, and her affairs went smoothly and miraculously. Her luggage was never delayed nor lost! Accommodations were always ready for her at the best hotels; and she had perfect service wherever she went. She returned to New York. Knowing the language, she felt God was no longer necessary, so looked after her affairs in an ordinary manner.

Everything went wrong, her trunks delayed, amid inharmony and confusion. The student must form the habit of "practicing the Presence of God" every minute. "*In all thy ways acknowledge him;*" nothing is too small or too great.

Sometimes an insignificant incident may be the turning point in a man's life.

Robert Fulton, watching some boiling water, simmering in a tea kettle, saw a steamboat!

I have seen a student, often, keep back his demonstration, through resistance, or pointing the way.

He pins his faith to one channel only, and dictates just the way he desires the manifestation to come, which brings things to a standstill.

"*My way, not your way!*" is the command of Infinite Intelligence. Like all Power, be it steam or electricity, it must have a nonresistant engine or instrument to work through, and man is that engine or instrument.

Over and over again, man is told to "stand still." "Oh Judah, fear not; but to-morrow go out against them, for the Lord will be with you. You shall not need to fight this battle; set yourselves, stand ye still, and see the salvation of the Lord with you."

We see this in the incidents of the two thousand dollars coming to the woman through the landlord when she became *nonresistant* and *undisturbed*, and the woman who won the man's love "after all suffering had ceased."

The student's goal is *Poise! Poise is Power*, for it gives God-Power a chance to rush through man, to "will and to do Its good pleasure."

Poised, he thinks clearly, and makes "right decisions quickly." "He never misses a trick."

Anger blurs the visions, poisons the blood, is the root of many diseases, and causes wrong decision leading to failure.

It has been named one of the worst "sins," as its reaction is so harmful. The student learns that in metaphysics sin has a much broader meaning than in the old teaching. "Whatsoever is not of faith is sin."

He finds that fear and worry are deadly sins. They are inverted faith, and through distorted mental pictures, bring to pass the thing he fears. His work is to drive out these enemies (from the subconscious mind). "When Man is *fearless he is finished!*" Maeterlinck says, that "Man is God afraid."

So, as we read in the previous chapters: Man can only vanquish fear by walking up to the thing he is afraid of. When Jehoshaphat and his army prepared to meet the enemy, singing "Praise the Lord, for his mercy endureth forever," they found their enemies had destroyed each other, and there was nothing to fight.

For example: A woman asked a friend to deliver a message to another friend. The woman feared to give the message, as the reasoning mind said, "Don't get mixed-up in this affair, don't give that message."

She was troubled in spirit, for she had given her promise. At last, she determined to "walk up to the lion," and call on the law of divine protection. She met the friend to whom she was to deliver the message. She opened her mouth to speak it, when her friend said, "So-and-So has left town." This made it unnecessary to give the message, as the situation depended upon the person being in town. As she was willing to do it, she was not obliged to; as she did not fear, the situation vanished.

The student often delays his demonstration through a belief in incompletion. He should make this statement:

"In Divine Mind there is only completion, therefore, my demonstration is completed. My perfect work, my perfect home, my perfect health." Whatever he demands are perfect ideas registered in Divine Mind, and must manifest, "under grace in a perfect way." He gives thanks he has already received on the invisible, and makes active preparation for receiving on the visible.

One of my students was in need of a financial demonstration. She came to me and asked why it was not completed.

I replied: "Perhaps, you are in the habit of leaving things unfinished, and the subconscious has gotten into the habit of not completing (as the without, so the within)."

She said, "You are right. I often *begin things* and never finish them.

"I'll go home and finish something I commenced weeks ago, and I know it will be symbolic of my demonstration."

So she sewed assiduously, and the article was soon completed. Shortly after, the money came in a most curious manner.

Her husband was paid his salary twice that month. He told the people of their mistake, and they sent word to keep it.

When man asks, *believing, he must receive, for God creates His own channels!*

I have been sometimes asked, "Suppose one has several talents, how is he to know which one to choose?" Demand to be shown definitely. Say: "Infinite Spirit, give me a definite lead, reveal to me my perfect self-expression, show me which talent I am to make use of now."

I have known people to suddenly enter a new line of work, and be fully equipped, with little or no training. So make the statement: "*I am fully equipped for the Divine Plan of my life,*" and be fearless in grasping opportunities.

Some people are cheerful givers, but bad receivers. They refuse gifts through pride, or some negative reason, thereby blocking their channels, and invariably find themselves eventually with little or nothing. For example: A woman who had given away a great deal of money, had a gift offered her of several thousand dollars. She refused to take it, saying she did not need it. Shortly after that, her finances were "tied up," and she found herself in debt for that amount. Man should receive gracefully the bread returning to him upon the water—freely ye have given, freely ye shall receive.

There is always the perfect balance of giving and receiving, and though man should give without thinking of returns, he violates law if he does not accept the returns which come to him; for all gifts are from God, man being merely the channel.

A thought of lack should never be held over the giver.

For example: When the man gave me the one cent, I did not say: "Poor man, he cannot afford to give me that." I saw him rich and prosperous, with his supply pouring in. It was this thought which brought it. If one has been a bad receiver, he must become a good one, and take even a postage stamp if it is given him, and open up his channels for receiving.

The Lord loveth a cheerful receiver, as well as a cheerful giver.

I have often been asked why one man is born rich and healthy, and another poor and sick.

Where there is an effect there is always a cause; there is no such thing as chance.

This question is answered through the law of reincarnation. Man goes through many births and deaths, until he knows the truth which sets him free.

He is drawn back to the earth plane through unsatisfied desire, to pay his Karmic debts, or to "fulfill his destiny."

The man born rich and healthy has had pictures in his subconscious mind, in his past life, of health and riches; and the poor and sick man, of disease and poverty. Man manifests, on any plane, the sum total of his subconscious beliefs.

However, birth and death are man-made laws, for the "wages of sin is death"; the Adamic fall in consciousness through the belief in two powers. The real man, spiritual man, is birthless and deathless! He never was born and has never died—"As he was in the beginning, he is now, and ever shall be!"

So through the truth, man is set free from the law of Karma, sin and death, and manifests the man made in "His image and likeness." Man's freedom comes through fulfilling his destiny, bringing into manifestation the Divine Design of his life.

His lord will say unto him: "Well done thou good and faithful servant, thou hast been faithful over a few things, I will make thee ruler over many things (death itself); enter thou into the joy of thy Lord (eternal life)."

10

DENIALS AND AFFIRMATIONS

Thou shalt also decree a thing,
and it shall be established unto thee.

All the good that is to be made manifest in man's life is already an accomplished fact in divine mind, and is released through man's recognition, or spoken word, so he must be careful to decree that only the Divine Idea be made manifest, for often, he decrees, through his "idle words," failure or misfortune.

It is, therefore, of the utmost importance, to word one's demands correctly, as stated in a previous chapter.

If one desires a home, friend, position or any other good thing, make the demand for the "divine selection."

For example: "Infinite Spirit, open the way for my right home, my right friend, my right position. I give thanks *it now manifests under grace in a perfect way.*"

The latter part of the statement is most important. For example: I knew a woman who demanded a thousand dollars. Her daughter was injured and they received a thousand dollars indemnity, so it did not come in a "perfect way." The demand should have been worded in this way: "Infinite Spirit, I give thanks that the one thousand dollars, which is mine by divine right, is now released, and reaches me under grace, in a perfect way."

As one grows in a financial consciousness, he should demand that the enormous sums of money, which are his by divine right, reach him under grace, in perfect ways.

It is impossible for man to release more than he thinks is possible, for one is bound by the limited expectancies of the subconscious. He must enlarge his expectancies in order to receive in a larger way.

Man so often limits himself in his demands. For example: A student made the demand for six hundred dollars, by a certain date. He did receive it, but heard afterwards, that he came very near receiving a thousand dollars, but he was given just six hundred, as the result of his spoken word.

"They limited the Holy One of Israel." Wealth is a matter of consciousness. The French have a legend giving an example of this. A poor man was walking along a road when he met a traveler, who stopped him and said: "My good friend, I see you are poor. Take this gold nugget, sell it, and you will be rich all your days."

The man was overjoyed at his good fortune, and took the nugget home. He immediately found work and became so prosperous that he did not sell the nugget. Years passed, and he became a very rich man. One day he met a poor man on the road. He stopped him and said: "My good friend, I will give you this gold nugget, which, if you sell, will make you rich for life." The mendicant took the nugget, had it valued, and found it was only brass. So we see, the first man became rich through feeling rich, thinking the nugget was gold.

Every man has within himself a gold nugget; *it is his consciousness of gold, of opulence, which brings riches into his life.* In making his demands, man begins at his *journey's end,* that is, he declares *he has already received. "Before ye call I shall answer."*

Continually affirming establishes the belief in the subconscious.

It would not be necessary to make an affirmation more than once if one had perfect faith! One should not plead or supplicate, but give thanks repeatedly, that he has received.

"The desert shall *rejoice* and blossom as the rose." This rejoicing which is yet in the desert (state of consciousness) opens the way for release. The Lord's Prayer is in the form of command and demand, "Give us this day our daily bread, and forgive us our debts as we forgive our debtors," and ends in praise, "For thine is the Kingdom and the Power and the Glory, forever. Amen." "Concerning the works of my hands, command ye me." So prayer is command and demand, praise and thanksgiving. The student's work is in making himself believe that "with God all things are possible."

This is easy enough to state in the abstract, but a little more difficult when confronted with a problem. For example: It was necessary for a woman to demonstrate a large sum of money within a stated time. She knew she must *do something* to get a realization (for realization is manifestation), and she demanded a "lead."

She was walking through a department store, when she saw a very beautiful pink enamel paper cutter. She felt the "pull" towards it. The thought came. "I haven't a paper cutter good enough to open letters containing large checks."

So she bought the paper cutter, which the reasoning mind would have called an extravagance. When she held it in her hand, she had a flash of a picture of herself opening an envelope containing a large check, and in a few weeks, she received the money. The pink paper cutter was her bridge of active faith.

Many stories are told of the power of the subconscious when directed in faith.

For example: A man was spending the night in a farmhouse. The windows of the room had been nailed down, and in the middle of the night he felt suffocated and made his way in the dark to the window. He could not open it, so he smashed the pane with his fist, drew in draughts of fine fresh air, and had a wonderful night's sleep.

The next morning, he found he had smashed the glass of a bookcase and the window had remained closed during the whole night. He had *supplied himself with oxygen, simply by his thought of oxygen*.

When a student starts out to demonstrate, he should never turn back. "Let not that man who wavers think that he shall receive anything of the Lord."

A student once made this wonderful statement, "When I ask the Father for anything, I put my foot down, and I say: Father, I'll take nothing less than I've asked for, but more!" So man should never compromise: "Having done all—Stand." This is sometimes the most difficult time of demonstrating. The temptation comes to give up, to turn back, to compromise.

"He also serves who only stands and waits."

Demonstrations often come at the eleventh hour because man then lets go, that is, stops reasoning, and Infinite Intelligence has a chance to work.

"Man's dreary desires are answered drearily, and his impatient desires, long delayed or violently fulfilled."

For example: A woman asked me why it was she was constantly losing or breaking her glasses.

We found she often said to herself and others with vexation, "I wish I could get rid of my glasses." So her impatient desire was violently fulfilled. What she should have demanded was perfect eye-sight, but what she registered in the subconscious was simply the impatient desire to be rid of her glasses; so they were continually being broken or lost.

Two attitudes of mind cause loss: depreciation, as in the case of the woman who did not appreciate her husband, or *fear of loss*, which makes a picture of loss in the subconscious.

When a student is able to let go of his problem (cast his burden) he will have instantaneous manifestation.

For example: A woman was out during a very stormy day and her umbrella was blown inside-out. She was about to make a call on some people whom she had never met and she did not wish to make her first appearance with a dilapidated umbrella. She could not throw it away, as it did not belong to her. So in desperation, she exclaimed: "Oh, God, you take charge of this umbrella, I don't know what to do."

A moment later, a voice behind her said: "Lady, do you want your umbrella mended?" There stood an umbrella mender.

She replied, "Indeed, I do."

The man mended the umbrella, while she went into the house to pay her call, and when she returned, she had a good umbrella. So there is always an umbrella mender at hand, on man's pathway, when one puts the umbrella (or situation) in God's Hands.

One should always follow a denial with an affirmation.

For example: I was called on the 'phone late one night to treat a man whom I had never seen. He was apparently very ill. I made the statement: "I deny this appearance of disease. It is unreal, therefore cannot register in his consciousness; this man is a perfect idea in Divine Mind, pure substance expressing perfection."

There is no time or space, in Divine Mind, therefore the word reaches instantly its destination and does not "return void." I have treated patients in Europe and have found that the result was instantaneous.

I am asked so often the difference between visualizing and visioning. Visualizing is a mental process governed by the reasoning or conscious mind; visioning is a spiritual process, governed by intuition, or the superconscious mind. The student should train his mind to receive these flashes of inspiration, and work out the "divine pictures," through definite leads. When a man can say, "I desire only that which God desires for me," his false desires fade from the consciousness, and a new set of blueprints is given him by the Master Architect, the God within. God's plan for each man transcends the limitation of the reasoning mind, and is always the square of life, containing health, wealth, love and perfect self-expression. Many a man is building for himself in imagination a bungalow when he should be building a palace.

If a student tries to force a demonstration (through the reasoning mind) he brings it to a standstill. "I will hasten it," saith the Lord. He should act only through intuition, or definite leads. "Rest in the Lord and wait patiently. Trust also in him, and he will bring it to pass."

I have seen the law work in the most astonishing manner. For example: A student stated that it was necessary for her to have a hundred dollars by the following day. It was a debt of vital importance which had to be met. I "spoke the word," declaring Spirit was "never too late" and that the supply was at hand.

That evening she 'phoned me of the miracle. She said that the thought came to her to go to her safety-deposit box at the bank to examine some papers. She looked over the papers, and at the bottom of the box, was a new one hundred dollar-bill. She was astounded, and said she knew she had never put it there, for she had gone through the papers many times. It may have been a materialization, as Jesus Christ materialized the loaves and fishes. Man will reach the stage where his "word is made flesh," or materialized, instantly. "The fields, ripe with the harvest," will manifest immediately, as in all of the miracles of Jesus Christ.

There is a tremendous power alone in the name Jesus Christ. It stands for *Truth Made Manifest*. He said, "Whatsoever ye ask the Father, in my name, he will give it to you."

The power of this name raises the student into the fourth dimension, where he is freed from all astral and psychic influences, and he becomes "unconditioned and absolute, as God Himself is unconditioned and absolute."

I have seen many healings accomplished by using the words, "In the name of Jesus Christ."

Christ was both person and principle; and the Christ within each man is his Redeemer and Salvation.

The Christ within, is his own fourth dimensional self, the man made in God's image and likeness. This is the self which has never failed, never known sickness or sorrow, was never born and has never died. It is the "resurrection and the life" of each man! "No man cometh to the Father save by the Son," means, that God, the Universal, working on the place of the particular, becomes the Christ in man; and the Holy Ghost, means God-in-action. So daily, man is manifesting the Trinity of Father, Son and Holy Ghost.

Man should make an art of thinking. The Master Thinker is an artist and is careful to paint only the divine designs upon the canvas of his mind; and he paints these pictures with masterly strokes of power and decision, having perfect faith that there is no power to mar their perfection and that they shall manifest in his life the ideal made real.

All power is given man (through right thinking) to bring his heaven upon his earth, and this is the *goal of the "Game of Life."*

The simple rules are fearless faith, nonresistance and love!

May each reader be now freed from that thing which has held him in bondage through the ages, standing between him and his own, and "know the Truth which makes him free"—free to fulfill his destiny, to bring into manifestation the "Divine Design of his life, Health, Wealth, Love and Perfect Self-Expression." "Be ye transformed by the renewing of your mind."

Denials and Affirmations

(For Prosperity)
God is my unfailing supply, and large sums of money come to me quickly, under grace, in perfect ways.

(For Right Conditions)
Every plan my Father in heaven has not planned, shall be dissolved and dissipated, and the Divine Idea now comes to pass.

(For Right Conditions)
Only that which is true of God is true of me, for I and the Father are ONE.

(For Faith)
As I am one with God, I am one with my good, for God is both the Giver and the Gift. I cannot separate the Giver from the gift.

(For Right Conditions)
Divine Love now dissolves and dissipates every wrong condition in my mind, body and affairs. Divine Love is the most powerful chemical in the universe, and dissolves everything which is not of itself!

(For Health)
Divine Love floods my consciousness with health, and every cell in my body is filled with light.

(For the Eyesight)
My eyes are God's eyes, I see with the eyes of spirit. I see clearly the open way; there are no obstacles on my pathway. I see clearly the perfect plan.

(For Guidance)
I am divinely sensitive to my intuitive leads, and give instant obedience to Thy will.

(For the Hearing)
My ears are God's ears, I hear with the ears of spirit. I am non-resistant and am willing to be led. I hear glad tidings of great joy.

(For Right Work)
I have a perfect work
In a perfect way;
I give a perfect service
For perfect pay.

(For Freedom from all Bondage)
I cast this burden on the Christ within, and I go free!